# A Core Methodist Hymnal

Hymn Texts in the Public Domain
Common to Historic Methodist Hymnals

edited by
Ted A. Campbell

with the research assistance of
Mara Richards Bim

Dallas: Tuckapaw Media
2024

# A Core Methodist Hymnal

Hymn Texts in the Public Domain
Common to Historic Methodist Hymnals

ISBN: 978-0-9820698-9-9

version 1.2,
30 July 2024

Annual Commemoration
of William Wilberforce (d. 1833)
and the Slavery Abolition Act of 1833

# Table of Contents

in memoriam conservandam

**LUCRETIAE**

matris carae

As my mother descended into Alzheimer's disease, she could no longer remember where she was or what we were doing or even the names of close friends. But she could still remember all the words of the hymns she learned as a girl. Christian songs shape Christians. They form our spiritual and intellectual lives. Reading and hearing and singing Christian songs form synaptic connections in our brains. In that sense, Christian songs even form our material bodies in Christian faith.

The purpose of this *Core Methodist Hymnal* is to offer a set of hymn texts in the public domain historically used by Wesleyan and Methodist communities in their officially adopted hymnals to form people today in a Wesleyan and Methodist way of being Christian. It is not intended as a hymnal to be used in congregations but rather as a devotional and teaching resource for those who seek a firmer foundation in the Wesleyan and Methodist way of being Christian.

Why do we need a *Core Methodist Hymnal?* Methodist people in the past learned a basic shape of Christian devotion and Christian teachings (doctrine) from hymn texts and by the systematic way in which hymns were laid out in hymnals. Approved by Methodist denominations, hymnals carried not only the faith of the hymns' authors and the preferences of pastors and music leaders, but they also reflected the consensus of the larger Christian community that authorized them as a hymnal. Methodist people like my mother may have never read the Articles of Religion or John Wesley's sermons, but they sang these hymn texts over and over, and the hymn texts shaped them as Christians.

But hymnals are no longer as frequently used or seen by Methodist congregations. Some prefer more contemporary Christian songs licensed through commercial licensing agencies. Others have hymnals but they remain unseen in favor of a projection system to show hymn texts. In either case, the congregation no longer sees hymns as they systematically present a church's teachings and spirituality.

Unlike more recent hymnals, this *Core Methodist Hymnal* contains:

- Hymn texts (words) only, no musical notation, like the earliest Methodist hymnals.

- Texts most frequently utilized in historic Wesleyan and Methodist churches. These are limited to texts written before 1910, but most are still in use on Methodist hymnals today.

- Selections of stanzas reflecting historic Methodist use and approval. (Some hymns originated as poems containing twenty or more stanzas, so churches had to decide which stanzas to use.)

- Texts that are now in the public domain. These texts (words) are free to use without copyright restrictions. The newest in here are from 1906. Oldies but goodies: a *Methodist Hymnal Classic.*

- Texts laid out in a typical Methodist order for hymnals including the praise of God, the praise of Jesus Christ, the praise of the Holy Spirit, the Christian community, the distinctly Methodist understanding of the "way of salvation" (preparing, justifying, and sanctifying grace, and a Christian death), and the coming reign of God.

We did not simply choose the hymns for this *Core Methodist Hymnal.* Using funds from the Albert C. Outler Chair of Wesley Studies at Perkins School of Theology, Southern Methodist University, I tasked graduate assistant Mara Richards Bim (MDiv) with studying the contents of nine hymnals of Methodist denominations including British as well as American hymnals:

*A Collection of Hymns for the Use of the People Called Methodists* (1780, British and American)

*Hymnal of the Methodist Episcopal Church* (1878, American)

*The African Methodist Episcopal Hymn and Tune Book* (1902; American, from a historically Black US denomination)

The *Methodist Hymn-Book* (1904 British and Australian)

The *Methodist Hymnal* (1905, American, Methodist Episcopal and Methodist Episcopal, South)

The *Methodist Hymnal* (1935, American, three denominations that formed the Methodist Church in 1939)

The *Methodist Hymnal* (1966; American, rebranded after 1968 as the *Book of Hymns* of The United Methodist Church)

The *United Methodist Hymnal* (1989, American)

The *A.M.E. Zion Bicentennial Hymnal* (1996, from a historically Black US denomination)

By consulting these historic hymn compilations, Ms Bim prepared a detailed spreadsheet by which she identified 124 hymn texts prior to the 1930s included in seven of the nine hymnals she studied. She identified 78 more hymn texts common to six of the nine hymnals and then a further 121 hymn texts common to at least five out of the nine hymnals. I'm deeply grateful for her work on this project.

The selection of hymns in this *Common Methodist Hymnal* began with the hymn texts common to seven of the nine hymnals we have documented, but I eliminated a few, like Isaac Watts's version of Psalm 100, "Before Jehovah's Awful Throne" because it so very closely parallels another paraphrase of Psalm 100, that of William Kethe, "All people that on earth do dwell..." I also left out "My Country, 'Tis of Thee" which has specific reference to the United States and might confuse British Methodists who are accustomed to singing "God Save the King" to the same tune. I'm leaving national songs out of a *Core Methodist Hymnal*.

Our identification of the hymns from seven-of-nine Methodist hymnals yielded an initial set of 119 hymn texts all written before 1900. These are heavy on hymns by Charles Wesley and Isaac Watts and other well-known eighteenth-century and nineteenth-century hymn writers, though they do include hymn texts by three women: Charlotte Elliott ("Just

As I Am"), Annie S. Hawks ("I Need Thee Every Hour"), and Cecil Frances *née* Humphries Alexander ("Jesus Calls Us").

I found, however, that the range of hymn texts that fell within those common to seven-of-nine hymnals were so weighted toward the earlier hymn texts that they did not include many hymn texts in the public domain that appeared in the late 1800s and the very early 1900s and I have added seven additional hymn texts to address two prominent omissions from this period.

In the first place, the hymn texts from seven-of-nine Methodist hymnals did not include any of the texts in the public domain by the prolific Methodist hymn writer Frances Jane *née* Crosby van Alstyne (1820-1915) who wrote under a number of names, most prominently "Fanny Crosby," and whose hymns appeared very prominently in later Methodist hymnals. I have added three of her most prominent hymn texts including "Pass Me Not, O Gentle Savior" which appeared in six out of the nine hymnals we surveyed and two texts that appeared in five of the nine hymnals: "Blessed Assurance" and "Rescue the Perishing."

In the second place, our seven-of-nine standard did not include hymn texts in the public domain by African-American hymn authors. I have added four additional hymn texts in the public domain from Methodist pastor and poet Charles Albert Tindley (1851-1933) including "When the Storms of Life are Raging, Stand by Me."

Like earlier Methodist hymnals, this *Core Methodist Hymnal* is laid out in a systematic way that follows the earlier hymnals' consistent outline. In introducing the very first Methodist hymnal in 1780, *A Collection of Hymns for the Use of the People Called Methodists*, John Wesley wrote:

> The hymns are not carelessly jumbled together, but carefully ranged under proper heads, according to the experience of real Christians. So that this book is in effect a little body of experimental [experiential] and practical divinity.

In keeping with this way of forming Methodist Christians by singing and hearing and reading hymns, the *Core Methodist Hymnal* has a systematic structure based on that of earlier

Methodist hymnals. The center of this structure is a pattern called "The Way of Salvation" involving preparing, justifying, and sanctifying grace."

Reading hymns sometimes gives different insights than singing them or hearing them. The singer has multiple tasks occurring simultaneously: she has to keep track of musical notation as well as the words. Those of us who grew up singing hymns to music can scarcely read them without thinking of the tunes, but reading hymns without music sometimes reveals nuances—sometimes revealed just by punctuation marks—that one might miss while singing. But I do encourage you to read out loud and to sing the hymns as well: the sound is a teacher that illuminates the meaning of a text.

The hymns included here often use English forms that are now archaic but which were part of a devotional language for English-speaking Protestants. Here are some elements of these traditional forms:

> Older hymns often address God using the second-person singular pronoun *thou* which in historic English was a more informal word used in a family setting or between close friends in contrast to "you," which in was more formal. An example: "from everlasting thou art God..." The use of *thou* suggested familiarity and closeness even in speaking to God.

> The pronoun *thou* was connected to verb forms ending with -*st* or -*est* as in, "thou mayest smile at all thy foes..." The word *thee* was used as the object of a sentence or a preposition, as in: "...in thee do we trust."

> In the older use, singular nouns were used with verb forms ending in -*th* or -*eth* as in: "He leadeth me..."

> The second-person plural pronoun was *ye*: "Come ye before him and rejoice!" *Ye* can be thought of as an older equivalent of the contemporary informal second-person plural pronoun *y'all* used in some US dialects today. *Ye* always denoted more than one person.

In keeping with the historic nature of this project, I have not altered hymns for inclusive language. It would be jarring in my view to have *thee* and *thou* language together with contemporary inclusive language, though in the notes I have pointed to some of the issues and I give reference to some alternative language for the hymns.

This *Core Methodist Hymnal* shows the "meter" for each hymn: a count of syllables line-by-line. You can use this to find tunes that will work for each hymn. For example, a hymn marked as "8 6 8 6 (Common Meter)" has stanzas with four lines: the first line has eight syllables, the second line six syllables, the third line eight syllables, the fourth line six syllables. You can sing almost any Common Meter hymn to the tune we traditionally use for "Amazing Grace." Try it, counting syllables on your fingers. Or you can use the tune for "The House of the Rising Sun" for the same group of Common Meter hymns, but of course with that tune you should sing it with a snarly blues sound.

I have added comments on each of the hymns, typically reflections on the meaning of the hymns and their place in learning the framework of a Wesleyan way of being Christian. Sometimes they are devotional thoughts, and sometimes they give my own contemporary reflections on the hymn texts. Some of these may involve slightly less-than-pious questions about the traditional meanings or wordings of the hymn texts.

Although these hymn texts are in the public domain, users should consistently honor and credit the authors of hymn texts. The hymn texts are great legacies: we must continue to acknowledge and celebrate their poetic inspiration.

I pray that you will find *A Core Methodist Hymnal* to be a means of grace, allowing you to pray with and to be formed by the songs of our Wesleyan and Methodist forebears: ☩

Methodist hymnals begin with the praise of God. They almost always began with some of the stanzas of a long poem that Charles Wesley composed in 1739 on the first anniversary of his conversion experience. The stanzas that John Wesley chose from this poem for the first Methodist hymnal in 1780 began with "O, for a thousand tongues to sing my dear Redeemer's praise!"

This section in Methodist hymnals is typically identified simply as "The Praise of God," not specifying the First Person of the Divine Trinity traditionally addressed as God the Father. But many of the hymns within this section as elsewhere are specifically Trinitarian, for example, the Thomas Ken doxology that begins "Praise God from whom all blessings flow" (see hymn 9 following).

1 O for a thousand tongues to sing
my great Redeemer's praise,
the glories of my God and King,
the triumphs of his grace!

2 My gracious Master and my God,
assist me to proclaim,
to spread through all the earth abroad
the honors of thy name.

3 Jesus! the name that charms our fears,
that bids our sorrows cease;
'tis music in the sinner's ears,
'tis life, and health, and peace.

4 He breaks the power of canceled sin,
he sets the prisoner free;
his blood can make the foulest clean;
his blood availed for me.

5 He speaks, and listening to his voice,
new life the dead receive;
the mournful, broken hearts rejoice,
the humble poor believe.

6 Hear him, ye deaf; his praise, ye dumb,
your loosened tongues employ;
ye blind, behold your savior come,
and leap, ye lame, for joy.

7 In Christ, your head, you then shall know,
shall feel your sins forgiven;
anticipate your heaven below,
and own that love is heaven.

Poet: Charles Wesley, 1739. Meter: 8 6 8 6 (Common Meter).

Originally a poem of eighteen stanzas, Methodist churches through the years have continued to refine which stanzas of the original poem they use for this hymn.

## 2 All People that on Earth do Dwell (Psalm 100)

1 All people that on earth do dwell,
sing to the LORD with cheerful voice;
him serve with mirth, his praise forth-tell;
come ye before him and rejoice!

2 Know that the LORD is God indeed;
without our aid he did us make;
we are his flock, he doth us feed,
and for his sheep he doth us take.

3 O enter then his gates with praise,
approach with joy his courts unto;
praise, laud, and bless his name always,
for it is seemly so to do.

4 Because the LORD our God is good;
his mercy is forever sure;
his truth at all times firmly stood
and shall from age to age endure.

Source: Psalm 100; English metrical paraphrase by William Kethe, 1561. Meter: 8 8 8 8 (Long Meter).

Hymns as we know them were a new development in the age of Isaac Watts and the Wesleys. Older Protestant communities had preferred only Psalms rendered in verse ("metrical Psalms") for Christian worship, like the version of Psalm 100 given here.

1 O God, our help in ages past,
our hope for years to come,
our shelter from the stormy blast,
and our eternal home.

2 Under the shadow of thy throne
thy saints have dwelt secure;
sufficient is thine arm alone,
and our defense is sure.

3 Before the hills in order stood,
or earth received its frame,
from everlasting thou art God,
to endless years the same.

4 A thousand ages in thy sight
are like an evening gone,
short as the watch that ends the night
before the rising sun.

5 Time, like an ever-rolling stream
bears all its sons away;
they fly forgotten, as a dream
dies at the opening day.

6 O God, our help in ages past,
our hope for years to come,
be thou our guard while life shall last,
and our eternal home!

Poet: Psalm 90; English metrical paraphrase by Isaac Watts, 1719. Meter: 8 6 8 6 (Common Meter).

Psalms like this one have no specific Christian references (at least in their Old Testament original forms) and can sometimes be used in inter-religious worship, that is worship that might include Jews and Muslims and other believers in God as well as Christians.

1 O worship the King all-glorious above,
O gratefully sing his power and his love:
our shield and defender, the Ancient of Days,
pavilioned in splendor and girded with praise.

2 O tell of his might and sing of his grace,
whose robe is the light, whose canopy space.
His chariots of wrath the deep thunderclouds form,
and dark is his path on the wings of the storm.

3 Thy bountiful care, what tongue can recite?
It breathes in the air, it shines in the light;
it streams from the hills, it descends to the plain,
and sweetly distills in the dew and the rain.

4 Frail children of dust, and feeble as frail,
in thee do we trust, nor find thee to fail.
Thy mercies, how tender, how firm to the end,
our Maker, Defender, Redeemer, and Friend!

Poet: Robert Grant, 1833. Meter: 10 10 11 11.

St Paul wrote in his letter to the Romans: "Ever since the creation of the world [God's] eternal power and divine nature, invisible though they are, have been understood and seen through the things he has made" (Romans 1:20). Robert Grant develops this idea with poetic imagery: God's "canopy" is space, and "His chariots of wrath the deep thunderclouds form…"

1 Come, sound his praise abroad,
and hymns of glory sing;
JEHOVAH is the sovereign God,
the universal King.

2 He formed the deeps unknown;
he gave the seas their bound;
the watery worlds are all his own,
and all the solid ground.

3 Come, worship at his throne,
come, bow before the Lord;
we are his works and not our own,
he formed us by his word.

4 Today attend his voice,
nor dare provoke his rod:
come, like the people of his choice,
and own your gracious God.

Poet: Isaac Watts, 1719. Meter: 6 6 8 6 (Short Meter).

A call to worship God using the odd combination of the four letters of the unpronounced Name of God in the Hebrew scriptures (YHWH or JHVH) with the vowels for *Adonai* ("Lord"). The King James translation of the English Bible used small capital letters to signal the weirdness of this construction (JEHOVAH) as a way of conveying devotion to the mysterious Name.

1 Come, we that love the Lord,
and let our joys be known;
join in a song with sweet accord,
and thus surround the throne.

2 Let those refuse to sing
who never knew our God;
but children of the heavenly King
may speak their joys abroad.

3 The hill of Zion yields
a thousand sacred sweets
before we reach the heavenly fields,
or walk the golden streets.

4 Then let our songs abound,
and every tear be dry;
we're marching through Emmanuel's ground
to fairer worlds on high.

Isaac Watts, 1707. Meter: 6 6 8 6 (Short Meter).

A piece of hymn lore associated with this song—probably just an old preacher joke and unlikely to be documented—is that the evangelist George Whitefield was preaching in the American colonies and noted that paid singers did not help the congregation sing the hymns. He invited the congregation to join in singing Dr Watts's hymn "Heavenly Joy on Earth," and encouraged the choir especially to join them on the second stanza: "Let those refuse to sing who never knew our God…"!

1 God moves in a mysterious way
his wonders to perform;
he plants his footsteps in the sea
and rides upon the storm.

2 Deep in unfathomable mines
of never-failing skill;
he treasures up his bright designs,
and works his sovereign will.

3 Ye fearful saints, fresh courage take;
the clouds ye so much dread
are big with mercy and shall break
in blessings on your head.

4 Judge not the Lord by feeble sense,
but trust him for his grace;
behind a frowning providence
he hides a smiling face.

5 His purposes will ripen fast,
unfolding every hour;
the bud may have a bitter taste,
but sweet will be the flower.

6 Blind unbelief is sure to err,
and scan his work in vain;
God is his own interpreter,
and he will make it plain.

Poet: William Cowper, 1774. Meter: 8 6 8 6 (Common Meter).

William Cowper was John Newton's partner in producing the *Olney Hymns* (1779) which included Newton's hymn "Amazing Grace." The *Olney Hymns* were laid out in a pattern following the Way of Salvation as John Wesley's 1780 *Collection of Hymns for the Use of the People Called Methodists* would do in the next year.

1 Holy, holy, holy! Lord God Almighty!
Early in the morning our song shall rise to thee;
Holy, holy, holy! merciful and mighty!
God in three Persons, blessed Trinity!

2 Holy, holy, holy! all the saints adore thee,
casting down their golden crowns
    around the glassy sea;
cherubim and seraphim, falling down before thee,
which wert and art and evermore shalt be.

3 Holy, holy, holy! Though the darkness hide thee,
though the eye of sinful man
    thy glory may not see;
only thou art holy, there is none beside thee,
perfect in power, in love, and purity.

4 Holy, holy, holy! Lord God Almighty!
All thy works shall praise thy name
in earth and sky and sea;
Holy, holy, holy! Merciful and mighty!
God in three Persons, blessed Trinity!

Poet: Reginald Heber, 1826. Meter: 11 12 12 10.

Reginald Heber was the Anglican Bishop of Calcutta (Kolkata) who reflected the High Church culture revived in Anglican churches of his age.
In this hymn he celebrated the three Persons of the Divine Trinity,
though they remain unnamed in the hymn. Methodists valued his devotional poetry and incorporated several hymns (three in this hymnal)
that he authored.

Praise God from whom all blessings flow.
Praise him, all creatures here below.
Praise him above, ye heavenly host.
Praise Father, Son, and Holy Ghost.
Amen.

Poet: Thomas Ken, 1674. Meter: 8 8 8 8 (Long Meter).

This traditional Trinitarian blessing has been consistently used in historic Methodist churches. A contemporary version with less gender-exclusive language for the three divine Persons by Gilbert Viera is given in *The United Methodist Hymnal* (1987, no. 94).

## 10 The God of Abraham Praise

1 The God of Abraham praise,
who reigns enthroned above;
ancient of everlasting days,
and God of love;
JEHOVAH, great I AM!
by earth and heaven confessed:
I bow and bless the sacred name forever blest.

2 The great I AM has sworn;
I on this oath depend.
I shall, on eagle wings upborne,
to heaven ascend.
I shall behold God's face;
I shall God's power adore,
and sing the wonders of God's grace forevermore.

3 The heavenly land I see,
with peace and plenty blest;
a land of sacred liberty,
and endless rest.
There milk and honey flow,
and oil and wine abound,
and trees of life forever grow with mercy crowned.

4 The God who reigns on high
the great archangels sing,
and "Holy, holy, holy!" cry,
"Almighty King!
who was, and is, the same,
and evermore shall be:
JEHOVAH, LORD, the great I AM, we worship thee!"

Source: Daniel Ben Judah, 14th Century; English paraphrase by Thomas Olivers. Meter: 6 6 8 4 (doubled).

This hymn builds on the poetry of a Jewish author, invoking not only the unpronounced divine name as JEHOVAH but also the meaning of the divine name "I AM" revealed to Moses in Exodus 3:14.

1 From all that dwell below the skies,
let the Creator's praise arise.
Let the Redeemer's name be sung
through every land by every tongue.

2 Eternal are thy mercies Lord.
Eternal truth attends thy Word.
Thy praise shall sound from shore to shore
till suns shall rise and set no more

Isaac Watts 1719. Meter: 8 8 8 8 (Long Meter).

A lay Methodist, Isaac B. Webb, recorded in his pencil-written diary that the first Christian worship service (of any denomination) in what is now the Dallas area of Texas was led by itinerant elder Thomas Brown at Farmer's Branch on Sunday, March 19, 1844, and it began with this hymn sung to the tune HEBRON. It is an apt song for a new Christian mission: "Let the Redeemer's name be sung through every land by every tongue." (Webb's diary, in the DeGolyer Library at Southern Methodist University.)

1 The Lord JEHOVAH reigns,
his throne is built on high;
the garments he assumes
are light and majesty:
his glories shine with beams so bright
no mortal eye can bear the sight.

2 The thunders of his hand
keep the wide world in awe;
his wrath and justice stand
to guard his holy law;
and where his love resolves to bless
his truth confirms and seals his grace.

3 Through all his ancient works
amazing wisdom shines,
confounds the powers of hell
and breaks their cursed designs;
strong is his arm, and shall fulfil
his great decrees, his sovereign will.

4 And can this mighty King
of glory condescend?
And will he write his name
my Father and my friend?
I love his name, I love his word;
join, all my powers, and praise the Lord.

Poet: Isaac Watts, 1709. Meter: 6 6 6 6 8 8.

Watts's hymn begins by speaking of the unimaginable distance between God and human beings, and yet concludes with the aspiration
to know God as "my Father and my friend."

1 Guide me, O thou great JEHOVAH,
pilgrim through this barren land;
I am weak, but thou art mighty;
hold me with thy powerful hand.
Bread of heaven, bread of heaven,
feed me now and evermore! [repeat]

2 Open now the crystal fountain,
where the healing waters flow.
Let the fire and cloudy pillar
lead me all my journey through.
Strong deliverer, strong deliverer,
be thou still my strength and shield! [repeat]

3 When I tread the verge of Jordan,
bid my anxious fears subside.
Death of death, and hell's destruction!
Land me safe on Canaan's side.
Songs of praises, songs of praises
I will ever give to thee! [repeat]

Poet: William Williams of Pantycelyn, 1745, translated into English by his brother Peter Williams. Meter: 8 7 8 7 8 7.

Williams Pantycelyn (pronounced like *pant-uh-kéllen*) as he is known in Wales by the name of his place of ministry was the great Welsh poet of the Evangelical Revival, and this hymn is regarded as his masterpiece. When his brother Peter translated the poem into English, he changed his brother's word *Arglwydd* (simply "Lord") into "JEHOVAH." When sung with the customary tune CWM RHONDDA, the last line of each stanza is repeated.

1 Come, ye thankful people, come,
raise the song of harvest home;
all is safely gathered in,
ere the winter storms begin.
God our Maker doth provide
for our wants to be supplied;
come to God's own temple, come,
raise the song of harvest home.

2 All the world is God's own field,
fruit as praise to God we yield;
wheat and tares together sown
are to joy or sorrow grown;
first the blade and then the ear,
then the full corn shall appear;
Lord of harvest, grant that we
wholesome grain and pure may be.

3 For the Lord our God shall come,
and shall take the harvest home;
from the field shall in that day
all offenses purge away,
giving angels charge at last
in the fire the tares to cast;
but the fruitful ears to store
in the garner evermore.

4 Even so, Lord, quickly come,
bring thy final harvest home;
gather thou thy people in,
free from sorrow, free from sin,
there, forever purified,
in thy presence to abide.
Come! with all thine angels, come!
raise the glorious harvest home.

Poet: Henry Alford, 1844. Meter: 7 7 7 7 doubled.

This hymn is especially used for Thanksgiving and Harvest festivals,
envisioning God's people as God's own good harvest.

1 On Jordan's stormy banks I stand,
and cast a wishful eye
to Canaan's fair and happy land,
where my possessions lie.

Refrain:
I am bound for the promised land,
I am bound for the promised land.
O, who will come and go with me?
I am bound for the promised land.

2 O'er all those wide extended plains
shines one eternal day;
there God the Son forever reigns,
and scatters night away. [Refrain]

3 No chilling winds or poisonous breath
can reach that healthful shore;
sickness and sorrow, pain and death,
are felt and feared no more. [Refrain]

4 When I shall reach that happy place,
I'll be forever blest,
for I shall see my Father's face,
and in his bosom rest. [Refrain]

Poet: Samuel Stennett, 1787. Meter: 8 6 8 6 (Common Meter) with refrain. The refrain is a nineteenth-century addition.

Hymns favored by Methodists sometimes employed highly personal and even erotic imagery to express the union of a Christian soul with God: in this case, "I shall see my Father's face and in his bosom rest." John Wesley sometimes objected to Charles's use of these kinds of images. But Methodists stand in a long tradition of Christian piety that recognized human affection as an analogy—perhaps the closest analogy—for human love for God.

Methodist hymnals continue with the praise of Jesus Christ. Like other Christians, we praise Jesus Christ as the Second Person of the Divine Trinity who became flesh (incarnate) for us and lived and died and rose again from the dead. We praise Jesus Christ as fully human and fully God.

The order of hymns in this section follows the sequence of Methodist hymnals with an initial group of hymns in general praise of Christ, and then hymns celebrating the particular events and moments in the life of Christ in the order of the primitive Christian message (I Corinthians 15:3-4), early Christian creeds like the Apostles' Creed, and in the Gospel books of the New Testament. This order also follows the yearly seasons of Advent (prophecies of the coming of Christ), Christmas (the birth of Jesus from the Blessed Virgin Mary), Epiphany (celebrating the revelation of Christ to the whole world), Lent (celebrating our Savior's suffering and death) and Easter (celebrating Christ's resurrection from the dead).

1 Christ, whose glory fills the skies,
Christ, the true, the only light,
sun of righteousness, arise,
triumph o'er the shade of night;
day-spring from on high, be near;
day-star, in my heart appear.

2 Dark and cheerless is the morn
unaccompanied by thee;
joyless is the day's return,
till thy mercy's beams I see,
till they inward light impart,
glad my eyes, and warm my heart.

3 Visit then this soul of mine,
pierce the gloom of sin and grief;
fill me, radiancy divine,
scatter all my unbelief;
more and more thyself display,
shining to the perfect day.

Poet: Charles Wesley, 1740. Meter: 7 7 7 7 7 7.

A simple song appropriate to morning worship praising Christ as God's
"true light, which enlightens everyone" (St John 1:9).

1 Jesus, the very thought of thee
with sweetness fills the breast;
but sweeter far thy face to see,
and in thy presence rest.

2 O hope of every contrite heart,
O joy of all the meek,
to those who fall, how kind thou art!
How good to those who seek!

3 But what to those who find? Ah, this
nor tongue nor pen can show;
the love of Jesus, what it is,
none but his loved ones know.

4 Jesus, our only joy be thou,
as thou our prize wilt be;
Jesus, be thou our glory now,
and through eternity.

Source: Attributed to St Bernard of Clairvaux, 12th Century AD; translated into English stanza by John B. Dykes, 1866. Meter: 8 6 8 6 (Common Meter).

This hymn attributed to a medieval poem by St Bernard of Clairvaux speaks of Christ with deep and personal affection, Christ whose presence "with sweetness fills the breast."

1 Come, thou long expected Jesus,
born to set thy people free;
from our fears and sins release us,
let us find our rest in thee.
Israel's strength and consolation,
hope of all the earth thou art;
dear desire of every nation,
joy of every longing heart.

2 Born thy people to deliver,
born a child and yet a King,
born to reign in us forever,
now thy gracious kingdom bring.
By thine own eternal spirit
rule in all our hearts alone;
by thine all sufficient merit,
raise us to thy glorious throne.

Poet: Charles Wesley, 1744. Meter: 8 7 8 7 doubled.

This is a favorite Advent hymn for Protestants though Catholics object
to the phrase "thine all sufficient merit." To Protestants, these words
means that we need no "merit" but Christ's merit. To Catholics, though,
it seems to rule out that God can grant some kind of "merit" to human
beings. It might be one of those many cases where we need to ask each
other more carefully what we mean by the words we sing.

## 19  Hail to the Lord's Anointed

1 Hail to the Lord's Anointed,
great David's greater Son!
Hail in the time appointed,
his reign on earth begun!
He comes to break oppression,
to set the captive free;
to take away transgression,
and rule in equity.

2 He comes with succor speedy
to those who suffer wrong;
to help the poor and needy,
and bid the weak be strong;
to give them songs for sighing,
their darkness turn to light,
whose souls, condemned and dying,
are precious in his sight.

3 He shall come down like showers
upon the fruitful earth;
love, joy, and hope, like flowers,
spring in his path to birth.
Before him on the mountains,
shall peace, the herald, go,
and righteousness, in fountains,
from hill to valley flow.

4 To him shall prayer unceasing
and daily vows ascend;
his kingdom still increasing,
a kingdom without end.
The tide of time shall never
his covenant remove;
his name shall stand forever;
that name to us is Love.

Poet: James Montgomery, 1821 (Psalm 72). Meter: 7 6 7 6 doubled.

James Montgomery has used a Royal Psalm (Psalm 72) to speak of Christ's coming (advent!) as the Anointed One.

1 "Hark!" the herald angels sing,
"Glory to the newborn King:
peace on earth, and mercy mild,
God and sinners reconciled!"
Joyful, all ye nations, rise,
join the triumph of the skies;
with the angelic hosts proclaim,
"Christ is born in Bethlehem!"

[Refrain:]
"Hark!" the herald angels sing,
"Glory to the newborn King!"

2 Christ, by highest heaven adored,
Christ, the everlasting Lord,
late in time behold him come,
offspring of the virgin's womb:
veiled in flesh the godhead see;
hail the incarnate deity,
pleased with us in flesh to dwell,
Jesus, our Immanuel. [Refrain]

3 Hail the heaven-born Prince of Peace!
Hail the sun of righteousness!
Light and life to all he brings,
risen with healing in his wings.
Mild he lays his glory by,
born that we no more may die,
born to raise us from the earth,
born to give us second birth. [Refrain]

Poet: Charles Wesley, 1739; altered by George Whitefield. Meter: 7 7 7 7 (doubled).

Charles Wesley originally wrote, "Hark! How all the welkin rings!" But "welkin" (meaning the dome of the heavens) was not a common word and George Whitefield mercifully made it, "Hark! The herald angels sing..." Poets have to work hard to make their words understandable, and sometimes churches have to revise the language of hymns to avoid misunderstandings and stereotypes.

### 21  Joy to the World! The Lord is Come!

1 Joy to the world, the Lord is come!
Let earth receive her King!
Let every heart prepare him room,
and heaven and nature sing.

2 Joy to the earth, the Savior reigns!
Let all their songs employ,
while fields and floods, rocks, hills, and plains
repeat the sounding joy.

3 No more let sins and sorrows grow,
nor thorns infest the ground;
He comes to make his blessings flow
far as the curse is found.

4 He rules the world with truth and grace,
and makes the nations prove
the glories of his righteousness
and wonders of his love.

Poet: Isaac Watts, 1719. Meter: 8 6 8 6 (Common Meter).

Isaac Watts's historic Christmas hymn has really nothing to do with a
bullfrog named Jeremiah.

1 Brightest and best of the sons of the morning,
dawn on our darkness and lend us your aid.
Star of the east, the horizon adorning,
guide where our infant redeemer is laid.

2 Cold on his cradle the dewdrops are shining;
low lies his head with the beasts of the stall.
Angels adore him in slumber reclining,
maker and monarch and Savior of all.

3 Shall we yield him in costly devotion
rarest of fragrances, tribute divine,
gems of the mountain and pearls of the ocean,
myrrh from the forest and gold from the mine?

4 Vainly we offer each ample oblation,
vainly with gifts would his favor secure.
Richer by far is the heart's adoration,
dearer to God are the prayers of the poor.

5 Brightest and best of the sons of the morning,
dawn on our darkness and lend us your aid.
Star of the east, the horizon adorning,
guide where our infant redeemer is laid.

Poet: Reginald Heber, 1811. Meter: 11 11 11 10.

Reginald Heber's poem praising the star that led the Magi to Christ was very popular in Methodist hymnals of the late 1800s and early 1900s when Protestants were just beginning to observe Christmas, but it hasn't fared as well since then. Maybe it had a catchy tune? Or maybe it's had more competition?

1 While shepherds watched their flocks by night,
all seated on the ground,
an angel of the Lord came down,
and glory shone around.

2 "Fear not," said he for mighty dread
had seized their troubled mind
"glad tidings of great joy I bring
to you and all mankind."

3 "To you, in David's town, this day
is born of David's line
a Savior, who is Christ the Lord;
and this shall be the sign:

4 "The heavenly babe you there shall find
to human view displayed,
all simply wrapped in swaddling clothes
and in a manger laid."

5 Thus spoke the angel. Suddenly
appeared a shining throng
of angels praising God, who thus
addressed their joyful song:

6 "All glory be to God on high,
and to the earth be peace;
to those on whom his favor rests
goodwill shall never cease."

Poet: Nahum Tate, 1700. Meter: 8 6 8 6 (Common Meter).

The shepherds represent ordinary folks in the Christmas story, which is why it's cool to let little kids in bathrobes represent them in Christmas pageants. It's good news: "...and to the earth be peace." Amen!

1 Behold the Savior of mankind
nailed to the shameful tree!
How vast the love that him inclined
to bleed and die for thee!

2 Hark, how he groans, while nature shakes,
and earth's strong pillars bend!
The temple's veil in sunder breaks;
the solid marbles rend.

3 'Tis done! the precious ransom's paid!
"Receive my soul!" he cries!
See where he bows his sacred head!
he bows his head and dies!

4 But soon he'll break death's envious chain,
and in full glory shine.
O Lamb of God, was ever pain,
was ever love, like thine?

Poet: Samuel Wesley, Sr., before 1709. Meter: 8 6 8 6 (Common Meter).

Samuel Wesley was the father of John and Charles Wesley and their
other brother and sisters. In this hymn, he echoes a theme that Charles
would take up again and again: Christ's victory over the powers of
death and the immense love Christ revealed in becoming human, even
to the point of a human death, for the sake of all humankind.

## 25 O Love Divine, What Hast Thou Done

1 O Love divine, what hast thou done?
The immortal God hath died for me!
The Father's co-eternal Son
bore all my sins upon the tree;
the immortal God for me hath died!
My Lord, my love is crucified.

2 Is crucified for me and you,
to bring us rebels back to God.
Believe, believe the record true,
we all are bought with Jesu's blood,
pardon for all flows from his side:
my Lord, my love, is crucified.

3 Then let us sit beneath the cross,
and gladly catch the healing stream,
all things for him account but loss,
and give up all our hearts to him;
of nothing think or speak beside:
my Lord, my love is crucified.

Poet: Charles Wesley 1742. Meter: 8 8 8 8 8 8 (Long Meter) tripled.

Here Charles Wesley echoed the sentiment of his father in the previous
hymn: the immensity of Christ's work as God who became human and
suffered and died for us. But Charles's verses are more intimate: "My
Lord, my love is crucified."

1 O sacred head, now wounded,
with grief and shame weighed down,
now scornfully surrounded
with thorns, thine only crown:
How pale thou art with anguish,
with sore abuse and scorn!
How does that visage languish
which once was bright as morn!

2 What thou, my Lord, hast suffered
was all for sinners' gain;
mine, mine was the transgression,
but thine the deadly pain.
Lo, here I fall, my Savior!
'Tis I deserve thy place;
look on me with thy favor,
vouchsafe to me thy grace.

3 What language shall I borrow
to thank thee, dearest friend,
for this, thy dying sorrow,
thy pity without end?
O make me thine forever!
And should I fainting be,
Lord, let me never, never
outlive my love for thee.

Source: A medieval poem in the tradition of devotional poetry addressed to the wounds and sufferings of Christ, in this case, addressed to the wound in Christ's head; sometimes attributed to St Bernard of Clairvaux, 12th century; translated into German by Paul Gerhardt in 1656, and then into English by James W. Alexander in 1830. Meter: 7 6 7 6 (doubled).

I found Paul Simon's "American Tune" wistful and beautiful, and I called my wife in to listen. "That's a hymn!" she said. "No it's not!" I said. But she was right. Expressing his grief over the result of the US presidential election of 1968, Paul Simon had used the sad and moving tune of the Passion Chorale to which this hymn is traditionally sung.

1 When I survey the wondrous cross
on which the Prince of glory died,
my richest gain I count but loss,
and pour contempt on all my pride.

2 Forbid it, Lord, that I should boast
save in the death of Christ, my God!
All the vain things that charm me most,
I sacrifice them through his blood.

3 See, from his head, his hands, his feet,
sorrow and love flow mingled down.
Did e'er such love and sorrow meet,
or thorns compose so rich a crown?

4 Were the whole realm of nature mine,
that were a present far too small.
Love so amazing, so divine,
demands my soul, my life, my all.

Poet: Isaac Watts, 1707. Meter: 8 8 8 8 (Long Meter).

Perhaps Isaac Watts's best-known hymn, "When I Survey the Wondrous Cross" celebrates Christ's self-offering with the challenge that
what we owe in return cannot be just an hour on Sunday morning or
ten percent of one's gross monthly income. What God desires is "my
soul, my life, my all."

1 Alas! and did my Savior bleed,
and did my Sovereign die!
Would he devote that sacred head
for sinners such as I?

[Refrain]:
At the cross, at the cross where I first saw the light,
and the burden of my heart rolled away:
it was there by faith I received my sight
and now I am happy all the day.

2 Was it for crimes that I have done,
he groaned upon the tree?
Amazing pity! Grace unknown!
And love beyond degree! [Refrain]

3 Well might the sun in darkness hide,
and shut its glories in,
when God, the mighty maker, died
for his own creature's sin. [Refrain]

4 Thus might I hide my blushing face
while his dear cross appears;
dissolve my heart in thankfulness,
and melt mine eyes to tears. [Refrain]

5 But drops of tears can ne'er repay
the debt of love I owe.
Here, Lord, I give myself away;
'tis all that I can do. [Refrain]

Poet: Isaac Watts, 1707. Meter 8 6 8 6 (Common Meter) with refrain.
The refrain "At the cross, at the cross..." was added later.

Watts again echoes the theme of what we owe in response to Christ's
becoming human and suffering and dying on our behalf: No deals, no
compromises, no excuses: "Here Lord, I give myself away..."

## 29  Am I a Soldier of the Cross

1 Am I a soldier of the cross,
a follower of the Lamb,
and shall I fear to own his cause,
or blush to speak his name?

2 Must I be carried to the skies
on flowery beds of ease,
while others fought to win the prize,
and sailed through bloody seas?

3 Are there no foes for me to face?
Must I not stem the flood?
Is this vile world a friend to grace,
to help me on to God?

4 Sure I must fight, if I would reign;
increase my courage, Lord!
I'll bear the toil, endure the pain,
supported by thy word.

5 The saints in all this glorious war
shall conquer, though they die;
they see the triumph from afar
by faith's discerning eye.

6 When that illustrious day shall rise,
and all thine armies shine
in robes of victory through the skies,
the glory shall be thine.

Poet: Isaac Watts, 1724 I Corinthians 16:13). Meter: 8 6 8 6 (Common Meter).

Watts's hymn uses a military metaphor as many hymns do. But Christian soldiers are weird soldiers. They conquer by turning the cheek and following Christ who gave himself up: they "conquer, though they die..." Like Christ.

1 "Christ the Lord is risen today," Alleluia!
earth and heaven in chorus say. Alleluia!
Raise your joys and triumphs high, Alleluia!
sing, ye heavens, and earth reply. Alleluia!

2 Love's redeeming work is done, Alleluia!
fought the fight, the battle won. Alleluia!
Death in vain forbids him rise. Alleluia!
Christ has opened paradise. Alleluia!

3 Lives again our glorious King! Alleluia!
Where, O death, is now thy sting? Alleluia!
Once he died our souls to save, Alleluia!
where's thy victory, boasting grave? Alleluia!

4 Soar we now where Christ has led, Alleluia!
following our exalted Head. Alleluia!
Made like him, like him we rise! Alleluia!
Ours the cross, the grave, the skies! Alleluia!

5 Hail the Lord of earth and heaven! Alleluia!
Praise to thee by both be given. Alleluia!
Thee we greet triumphant now: Alleluia!
Hail the Resurrection, thou! Alleluia!

6 King of glory, soul of bliss! Alleluia!
Everlasting life is this: Alleluia!
thee to know, thy power to prove, Alleluia!
thus to sing, and thus to love, Alleluia!

Poet: Charles Wesley, 1739. Original Meter: 7 7 7 7.

Charles Wesley's original poem did not include the alleluias at the end
of each line. These were added in the 1800s when Protestants began
to follow the medieval Western Christian custom of refraining from
saying "Alleluia" during Lent and then emphasizing "Alleluia!" at Easter.
Adding the alleluias changes the meter from 7 7 7 7 to 11 11 11 11.

1 The day of resurrection!
Earth, tell it out abroad;
the Passover of gladness,
the Passover of God.
From death to life eternal,
from earth unto the sky,
our Christ hath brought us over,
with hymns of victory.

2 Our hearts be pure from evil,
that we may see aright
the Lord in rays eternal
of resurrection light;
and listening to his accents,
may hear, so calm and plain,
his own "All hail!" and, hearing,
may raise the victor strain.

3 Now let the heavens be joyful!
Let earth the song begin!
Let the round world keep triumph,
and all that is therein!
Let all things seen and unseen
their notes in gladness blend,
for Christ the Lord hath risen,
our joy that hath no end.

Poet: St John of Damascus, 8th Century AD; translated into English by John Mason Neale, 1862. Meter: 7 6 7 6 doubled.

In 1931 Swedish Bishop Gustav Aulén revived the medieval belief that emphasized Christ's victory over the forces of evil by offering himself as bait for Satan. But the resurrection was Satan's ultimate doom! *Christus Victor*, "Christ the Conqueror," was the title of Aulén's book. St John of Damascus's hymn given here is an early medieval expression of this perspective on Christ's work.

1 I know that my Redeemer lives,
and ever prays for me.
A token of his love he gives,
a pledge of liberty.

2 I find him lifting up my head;
he brings salvation near;
His presence makes me free indeed,
and he will soon appear.

3 He wills that I should holy be,
what can withstand his will?
The counsel of his grace in me
he surely shall fulfill.

4 Jesus, I hang upon thy word;
I steadfastly believe
thou wilt return and claim me, Lord,
and to thyself receive.

5 When God is mine and I am his,
of paradise possessed,
I taste unutterable bliss
and everlasting rest.

Poet: Samuel Medley, 1775. Meter: 8 6 8 6 (Common Meter).

This hymn offers a complementary perspective to the previous hymn of St John of Damascus. This one from Baptist minister Samuel Medley, a contemporary of John Wesley, emphasizes personal, heartfelt faith in the resurrection of Christ.

Catholic theologian Elizabeth A. Johnson wrote that theologians seem to get tired by the time they finally get around to the Holy Spirit. The original form of the Nicene Creed, she pointed out, ended abruptly with "And in the Holy Spirit" with nothing following (*She Who Is*, the section "Forgetting the Spirit," pp. 141-143). You might say the same thing about hymn writers: they don't seem to generate as much media about the Holy Spirit as they do about the Father and the Son.

But there is a small body of hymns about the work of the Holy Spirit beginning with the very first Methodist hymn collection of 1780. Four are given here based on what was commonly included in historic Methodist hymnals.

1 Come, Holy Spirit, heavenly Dove,
with all thy quickening powers;
kindle a flame of sacred love
in these cold hearts of ours.

2 O raise our thoughts from things below,
from vanities and toys;
then shall we with fresh courage go
to reach eternal joys.

3 Awake our souls to joyful songs;
let pure devotion rise,
till praise employs our thankful tongues,
and doubt forever dies.

4 Come, Holy Spirit, heavenly Dove,
with all thy quickening powers;
come, shed abroad a Savior's love,
and that shall kindle ours.

Poet: Isaac Watts, 1707, based on the Latin prayer *Veni, Sancte Spiritus* ("Come, Holy Spirit"). Meter: 8 6 8 6 (Common Meter).

An English version of the Latin Pentecost hymn "Come, Creator Spirit" was part of the Church of England's service of ordination. Isaac Watts wrote this poem hymn building on the tradition of *Veni, Sancte Spiritus*. Watts's hymn asks for the personal experience of the Spirit: "kindle a flame of sacred love in these cold hearts of ours."

1 Come, Holy Ghost, our hearts inspire,
let us thine influence prove;
source of the old prophetic fire,
fountain of life and love.

2 Come, Holy Ghost, for, moved by thee,
thy prophets wrote and spoke:
unlock the truth, thyself the key,
unseal the sacred book.

3 Expand thy wings, celestial Dove,
brood o'er our nature's night;
on our disordered spirits move,
and let there now be light.

4 God, through himself, we then shall know,
if thou within us shine;
and sound, with all thy saints below,
the depths of love divine.

Poet: Charles Wesley, 1740. Meter: 8 6 8 6 (Common Meter).

Following Watts, Charles Wesley used the beginning of the Pentecost and ordination hymn to link the fire of prophetic inspiration with the personal experience of the Spirit's presence: "...let us thine influence prove" (meaning "test" or "try").

1 O come and dwell in me,
Spirit of power within,
and bring the glorious liberty
from sorrow, fear, and sin.

2 Hasten the joyful day
which shall my sins consume,
when old things shall be done away,
and all things new become.

3 I want the witness, Lord,
that all I do is right,
according to thy mind and word,
well-pleasing in thy sight.

4 I ask no higher state;
indulge me but in this,
and soon or later then translate
to thine eternal bliss.

Poet: Charles Wesley, 1762. Meter: 6 6 8 6 (Short Meter).

Charles Wesley asks the Holy Spirit in these verses to give "the witness that all I do is right," that is, the witness of the Holy Spirit that confirms that we are acting according to the Spirit. Methodists would speak and sing of a two-fold witness to our gracious relationship with God: the direct witness of the Spirit that our sins have been forgiven, and the witness of changed lives that complements the direct witness of the Spirit.

1 O Spirit of the living God,
in all the fullness of your grace,
wherever human feet have trod,
descend upon our fallen race.

2 Give tongues of fire and hearts of love
to preach the reconciling word;
anoint with power from heaven above
whenever gospel truth is heard.

3 Let darkness turn to radiant light,
confusion vanish from your path;
those who are weak inspire with might:
let mercy triumph over wrath!

4 O Spirit of our God, prepare
the whole wide world the Lord to meet;
breathe out new life, like morning air,
till hearts of stone begin to beat.

5 Baptize the nations; far and near
the triumphs of the cross record;
till Christ in glory shall appear
and every race declare him Lord!

Poet: James Montgomery, 1823. Meter: 8 8 8 8 (Long Meter).

James Montgomery's hymn also invokes the Holy Spirit, asking for divine power to proclaim the message of the Gospel to the whole world.

Charles Wesley wrote volumes of poetry about Christian fellowship and John Wesley included some of these in the first Methodist hymn collection of 1780. The hymns in this section include meditations on the beauty of Christian fellowship, on the nature of the universal Christian church, the Methodist custom of covenant renewal, and the sacrament of the Lord's Supper. The section begins with hymns to open a Christian gathering and concludes with blessings for the ending of such a gathering.

1 And are we yet alive,
and see each other's face?
Glory and praise to Jesus give
for his redeeming grace.

2 Preserved by power divine
to full salvation here,
again in Jesus' praise we join,
and in his sight appear.

3 What troubles have we seen,
What conflicts have we passed,
Fightings without, and fears within,
Since we assembled last.

4 But out of all the Lord
hath brought us by his love.
And still he doth his help afford,
and hides our life above.

5 Then let us make our boast
of his redeeming power,
which saves us to the uttermost,
till we can sin no more.

6 Let us take up the cross
till we the crown obtain,
and gladly reckon all things loss,
so we may Jesus gain.

Poet: Charles Wesley, 1749. Meter: 6 6 8 6 (Short Meter).

This hymn is traditionally used to begin Methodist conferences. When an annual conference was only a gathering of itinerant (traveling) ministers, participants were never sure that they would be able "to see each other's face" when they next met. The expression "which saves us to the uttermost" refers to entire sanctification: see below under hymns of sanctifying grace.

1 Blest be the dear uniting love
that will not let us part;
our bodies may far off remove,
we still are one in heart.

2 Joined in one spirit to our Head;
where he appoints, we go,
and still in Jesus' footsteps tread,
and show his praise below.

3 O may we ever walk in him,
and nothing know beside,
nothing desire, nothing esteem,
but Jesus crucified!

4 Closer and closer let us cleave
to his beloved embrace;
expect his fulness to receive,
and grace to answer grace.

5 Partakers of the Savior's grace,
the same in mind and heart.
Nor joy, nor grief, nor time, nor place,
nor life, nor death can part.

Poet: Charles Wesley, 1742. Meter: 8 6 8 6 (Common Meter).

Charles Wesley's poem describes the love that binds Christians together with Christ and with each other, and continues whether we are
together or apart, in life and in death.

1 Jesus, united by thy grace,
and each to each endeared,
with confidence we seek your face,
and know our prayer is heard.

2 Help us to help each other, Lord,
each other's cross to bear,
let all their friendly aid extend,
and feel the other's care.

3 Up into you, our living head,
let us in all things grow,
till you have made us free indeed
and faithful here below.

4 Touched by the lodestone of your love,
let all our hearts unite;
let us toward each other move,
and move toward your light.

5 To thee, inseparably joined,
let all our spirits cleave;
O may we all the loving mind
that was in thee receive.

6 This is the bond of perfectness,
thy spotless charity;
O let us still, we pray, possess
the mind that was in thee.

Poet: Charles Wesley, 1742. Meter: 8 6 8 6 (Common Meter).

This hymn envisions Christ's love as a compass needle (a "lodestone")
that points us to God and to fellowship with each other. The word
"charity" here reflects the Latin word *caritas*, love in the sense of "dear-
ness" or "tenderness" to each other.

## 40 Lord, Dismiss Us with Thy Blessing

1 Lord, dismiss us with your blessing;
fill our hearts with joy and peace.
Let us each, your love possessing,
triumph in redeeming grace.
O refresh us, O refresh us,
traveling through this wilderness.

2 Thanks we give and adoration
for the gospel's joyful sound:
may the fruits of your salvation
in our hearts and lives abound!
Ever faithful, ever faithful
to your truth may we be found.

3 So whene'er the signal's given
us from earth to call away,
borne on angels' wings to heaven,
glad the summons to obey,
may we ever, may we ever
reign with Christ in endless day.

Poet: John Fawcett, 1773. Meter: 8 7 8 7 8 7.

The Wesleys' contemporary John Fawcett offers a hymn of blessing for the conclusion of a gathering, a prayer that the fellowship of Christ and the community will continue to refresh us beyond the gathering.

1 See, Israel's gentle Shepherd stands
with all-engaging charms;
Hark, how he calls the tender lambs,
and folds them in his arms!

2 "Permit them to approach," he cries,
"Nor scorn their humble name;
for 'twas to bless such souls as these
the Lord of angels came."

3 We bring them, Lord, in thankful hands,
and yield them up to thee;
joyful that we ourselves are Thine,
thine let our offspring be.

Poet: Philip Doddridge, 1755. Meter: 8 6 8 6 (Common Meter).

Recalling Jesus' ministry to children, Doddridge calls Christians to remember the central place of children in the church and in Christ's kingdom.

1 I love thy kingdom, Lord,
the house of thine abode,
the church our blest Redeemer saved
with his own precious blood.

2 I love thy church, O God:
her walls before thee stand,
dear as the apple of thine eye
and graven on thy hand.

3 For her my tears shall fall,
for her my prayers ascend;
to her my cares and toils be given,
'til toils and cares shall end.

4 Beyond my highest joy
I prize her heavenly ways,
her sweet communion, solemn vows,
her hymns of love and praise.

5 Sure as thy truth shall last,
to Zion shall be given
the brightest glories earth can yield,
and brighter bliss of heaven.

Poet: Timothy Dwight, 1800. Meter: 6 6 8 6 (Short Meter).

New England Congregationalist poet Timothy Dwight IV was the eighth president of Yale College. Here he offers a vision of the church as it should be: a vision of a sacred community that that loves "her sweet communion, solemn vows, her hymns of love and praise."

1 The church's one foundation is Jesus Christ, her Lord;
she is his new creation, by water and the word.
From heaven he came and sought her to be his holy bride;
with his own blood he bought her, and for her life he died.

2 Elect from every nation, yet one o'er all the earth,
her charter of salvation: one Lord, one faith, one birth.
One holy name she blesses, partakes one holy food,
and to one hope she presses, with every grace endued.

3 'Mid toil and tribulation, and tumult of her war,
she waits the consummation of peace forevermore;
till with the vision glorious her longing eyes are blest,
and the great church victorious shall be the church at rest.

4 Yet she on earth hath union with God the Three in One,
and mystic sweet communion
with those whose rest is won;
O happy ones and holy! Lord, give us grace that we
like them, the meek and lowly,
on high may dwell with thee.

Poet: Samuel John Stone, 1866. Meter: 7 6 7 6 doubled.

Anglican priest Samuel John Stone offers a vision of the Christian
church transcending space and time and reflecting on earth the mysti-
cal fellowship or communion between the three divine Persons of the
Holy Trinity.

1 Glorious things of thee are spoken,
Zion, city of our God.
He whose Word cannot be broken
formed thee for His own abode.
On the Rock of Ages founded,
what can shake thy sure repose?
With salvation's walls surrounded,
thou mayest smile at all thy foes.

2 See, the streams of living waters,
springing from eternal love,
well supply thy sons and daughters
and all fear of want remove.
Who can faint while such a river
ever flows their thirst to assuage?
Grace, which like the Lord, the Giver,
never fails from age to age.

3 'Round each habitation hovering,
see the cloud and fire appear
for a glory and a covering,
showing that the Lord is near.
Thus deriving from their banner
light by night and shade by day,
safe they feed upon the manna
which He gives them on their way.

4 Blessed inhabitants of Zion,
washed in our Redeemer's blood,
Jesus, whom our souls rely on,
makes us monarchs priests to God.
Us, by his great love, he raises
rulers over self to reign,
and as priests his solemn praises
we for thankful offering bring.

Poet: John Newton, 1779. Meter: 8 7 8 7 doubled.

Another of the *Olney Hymns* collection offers a vision of the church reflecting on earth the heavenly Jerusalem (Revelation 21).

1 Ye servants of God, your Master proclaim,
and publish abroad his wonderful name;
the name all-victorious of Jesus extol;
his kingdom is glorious and rules over all.

2 God ruleth on high, almighty to save;
though hid from our sight, his presence we have;
the great congregation his triumph shall sing,
ascribing salvation to Jesus our King.

3 "Salvation to God, who sits on the throne!"
let all cry aloud and honor the Son;
the praises of Jesus the angels proclaim,
fall down on their faces and worship the Lamb.

4 Then let us adore and give him his right:
all glory and power, all wisdom and might,
all honor and blessing with angels above
and thanks never ceasing and infinite love.

Poet: Charles Wesley, 1744. Meter: 10 10 11 11.

This hymn of Charles Wesley emphasizes the role of the church in proclamation of the name of Jesus, a name that in Hebrew carries the meaning, "God saves."

1 According to thy gracious word,
in meek humility,
this will I do, my dying Lord,
I will remember thee.

2 Thy body, broken for my sake,
my bread from heaven shall be;
thy testamental cup I take,
and thus remember thee.

3 Gethsemane can I forget?
Or there thy conflict see,
thine agony and bloody sweat,
and not remember thee?

4 When to the cross I turn mine eyes,
and rest on Calvary,
O Lamb of God, my sacrifice,
I must remember thee.

5 Remember thee, and all thy pains,
and all thy love to me:
when thou shalt in thy kingdom come,
Jesus, remember me.

Poet: James Montgomery, 1825. Meter: 8 6 8 6 (Common Meter).

James Montgomery's reference to "thy testamental cup" refers to receiving wine in the celebration of the Lord's Supper, fulfilling Jesus' words: "For as often as you eat this bread and drink the cup, you proclaim the Lord's death until he comes" (I Corinthians 11:26).

1 Bread of the world in mercy broken,
wine of the soul in mercy shed,
by whom the words of life were spoken,
and in whose death our sins are dead.

2 Look on the heart by sorrow broken,
look on the tears by sinners shed;
and be thy feast to us the token
that by thy grace our souls are fed.

Poet: Reginald Heber, 1827. Meter 9 8 9 8.

Remembering Christ's suffering by way of the communion elements, Reginald Heber offers a prayer that those whose hearts are broken by sadness may find healing in the sacrament.

1 Come, let us use the grace divine,
and all with one accord,
in a perpetual covenant join
ourselves to Christ the Lord;
Give up ourselves, thru Jesus' power,
his name to glorify;
and promise, in this sacred hour,
for God to live and die.

2 The covenant we this moment make
be ever kept in mind;
we will no more our God forsake,
or cast these words behind.
We never will throw off the fear
of God who hears our vow;
and if thou art well pleased to hear,
come down and meet us now.

3 Thee, Father, Son, and Holy Ghost,
let all our hearts receive,
present with thy celestial host
the peaceful answer give;
to each covenant the blood apply
which takes our sins away,
and register our names on high
and keep us to that day!

Poet: Charles Wesley, 1762. 8 6 8 6 (Common Meter) doubled.

This poem/hymn is associated with the Puritan and Methodist custom of the covenant renewal, invoking the three Persons of the divine Trinity to solemnize the promises made in this observance.

1 O thou, in whose presence my soul takes delight,
on whom in affliction I call;
my comfort by day, and my song in the night,
my hope, my salvation, my all.

2 Where dost thou, dear shepherd, resort with thy sheep,
to feed them in pastures of love?
Say, why in the valley of death should I weep,
or alone in this wilderness rove?

3 O why should I wander an alien from thee,
or cry in the desert for bread?
Thy foes will rejoice, when my sorrows they see,
and smile at the tears I have shed.

4 Restore, my dear Savior, the light of thy face,
thy soul-cheering comfort impart;
and let the sweet tokens of pardoning grace
bring joy to my desolate heart.

5 He looks! and ten thousands of angels rejoice,
and myriads wait for his word;
He speaks! and eternity, filled with his voice,
re-echoes the praise of the Lord.

Source: Psalm 23; Joseph Swain, 1791. Meter: 11 8 11 8.

Joseph Swain alludes to the Shepherd Psalm to envision the Lord's Supper as the Shepherd's own feeding of God's people in green pastures. The "sweet tokens of pardoning grace" in stanza 4 refer to the elements of the Lord's Supper.

1 Savior, again to thy dear name we raise
with one accord our parting hymn of praise.
Once more we bless thee ere our worship cease,
then, lowly bending, wait thy word of peace.

2 Grant us thy peace upon our homeward way;
with thee began, with thee shall end the day.
Guard thou the lips from sin, the hearts from shame,
that in this house have called upon thy name.

3 Grant us thy peace, Lord, through the coming night;
turn thou for us its darkness into light.
From harm and danger keep thy children free,
for dark and light are both alike to thee.

4 Grant us thy peace throughout our earthly life,
our balm in sorrow and our stay in strife.
Then, when thy voice shall bid our conflict cease,
call us, O Lord, to thine eternal peace.

Poet: John Ellerton, 1866. Meter: 10 10 10 10.

A hymn for the conclusion of worship with a prayer for peace and a
prayer that congregants will keep the solemn promises they have
made to God in the presence of the fellowship.

1 And let our bodies part,
to different climes repair;
inseparably joined in heart
the friends of Jesus are.

2 Jesus, the cornerstone
did first our hearts unite;
and still he keeps our spirits one
who walk with him in white.

3 O let us still proceed
in Jesus' work below,
and, following our triumphant Head,
to further conquest go.

4 O let our heart and mind
continually ascend,
that heaven of repose to find,
where all our labors end!

Poet: Charles Wesley, 1749. Meter: 6 6 8 6 (Short Meter).

Another prayer for the dismissal of a Christian fellowship, a prayer that
although "our bodies part," our souls remain in fellowship with each
other and with Christ.

1 Blest be the tie that binds
our hearts in Christian love;
the fellowship of kindred minds
is like to that above.

2 Before our Father's throne
we pour our ardent prayers;
our fears, our hopes, our aims are one,
our comforts and our cares.

3 We share our mutual woes,
our mutual burdens bear,
and often for each other flows
the sympathizing tear.

4 When we asunder part,
it gives us inward pain;
but we shall still be joined in heart,
and hope to meet again.

Poet: John Fawcett, 1782. Meter: 6 6 8 6 (Short Meter).

Musician and Christian worship scholar Roger Deschner told a story about a birthday party where the child being celebrated had requested a birthday pie rather than a birthday cake. One of the child's friends began singing at the top of his voice, "Blest be the pie that binds!" Sometimes even mis-remembered hymn lyrics can bring grace.

1 God be with you till we meet again;
loving counsels guide, uphold you,
may the Shepherd's care enfold you;
God be with you till we meet again.

Refrain:
Till we meet, till we meet,
till we meet at Jesus' feet.
Till we meet, till we meet,
God be with you till we meet again.

2 God be with you till we meet again;
unseen wings, protecting, hide you,
daily manna still provide you;
God be with you till we meet again. [Refrain]

3 God be with you till we meet again;
when life's perils thick confound you,
put unfailing arms around you;
God be with you till we meet again. [Refrain]

4 God be with you till we meet again;
keep love's banner floating o'er you,
smite death's threat'ning wave before you;
God be with you till we meet again. [Refrain]

Poet: Jeremiah E. Rankin, 1880. Meter: 98.89 with Refrain.

From some time in the 1800s it became popular to add refrains or choruses to songs to highlight central and recurring teachings or ideas.
This is a good example. Earlier poets like Isaac Watts and Charles Wesley would not have envisioned choruses like these and they were often
added to older hymns in the mid- to later 1800s. In this case, though,
the repeating refrain was part of Rankin's design.

## The Way of Salvation: Preparing Grace

One of the most distinctive traits of Wesleyan and Methodist communities of faith is their teaching of "the way of salvation," the progress of the Christian life leading to eternal life with Christ. John Wesley's sermons taught about the way of salvation, and Methodist hymnals from 1780 had a section of hymns following to the stages of the way of salvation.

John Wesley spoke of God's grace "prevening" (coming before) our believing in Christ. He used the term "preventing grace" to describe this, though the word "prevent" now means "to come before" something to *keep* it from happening. John and Charles Wesley meant the opposite: God's grace "coming before" something to *make* it happen. So the expression "preventing grace" is very problematic.

Theologians from the mid-twentieth century preferred to use the phrase *prevenient grace* to mean the same thing, God's grace prevening or "coming before" our believing in Christ and before any good work we might do. But "prevenient grace" sounds technical and rarefied. For this *Core Methodist Hymnal*, I'll use the expression "preparing grace": God's grace *preparing* us to believe in Christ and preparing us and the world to follow God's good ways.

1 Come, sinners, to the gospel feast,
let every soul be Jesus' guest.
Ye need not one be left behind
for God hath bidden all mankind.

2 Sent by my Lord, on you I call,
the invitation is to all.
Come, all the world! Come, sinner, thou!
All things in Christ are ready now.

3 Come, all ye souls by sin oppressed,
ye restless wanderers after rest,
ye poor, and maimed, and halt, and blind,
in Christ a hearty welcome find.

4 My message as from God receive:
Ye all may come to Christ and live.
O let His love your hearts constrain,
nor suffer him to die in vain.

5 See him set forth before your eyes,
That precious, bleeding sacrifice!
his offered benefits embrace,
and freely now be saved by grace!

Poet: Charles Wesley, 1747. Meter: 8 8 8 8 (Long Meter).

Charles Wesley's poem "The Great Supper" had 22 stanzas and was both an invitation to the Lord's Supper and also a call to sinners to turn to Christ. Methodist hymnals have generally selected stanzas such as these that focus on the call for repentance, but some hymnals have a selection of stanzas specifically for the celebration of the Lord's Supper (see *United Methodist Hymnal* 1989, 339 and 616).

Preparing grace is God's grace especially for those ("sinners") who think of themselves as unworthy of God. In Methodist theology, "the invitation is to all": no one is excluded from the call and grace of Christ.

1 Amazing grace! How sweet the sound!
That saved a wretch like me!
I once was lost, but now am found,
was blind, but now I see.

2 'Twas grace that taught my heart to fear,
and grace my fears relieved;
how precious did that grace appear
the hour I first believed!

3 Through many dangers, toils and snares
I have already come:
'tis grace has brought me safe thus far,
and grace will lead me home.

4 The Lord has promised good to me,
his word my hope secures;
he will my shield and portion be
as long as life endures.

5 Yea, when this flesh and heart shall fail,
and mortal life shall cease:
I shall possess, within the veil,
a life of joy and peace.

6 When we've been there ten thousand years,
bright shining as the sun,
we've no less days to sing God's praise
than when we'd first begun.

Poet: John Newton, 1779. Meter: 8 6 8 6 (Common Mater).

"Amazing Grace" covers all the elements of the "way of salvation": grace
"taught my heart to fear" (preparing grace); grace "my fears relieved"
(justifying grace), and grace "will lead me home" (sanctifying grace).
Newton's original poem had a gloomy apocalyptic ending stanza re-
placed in popular practice with the concluding stanza shown here. Like
a Psalm, the hymn has no specifically Christian language, which might
contribute to it remaining a perennial favorite in popular culture.

1 Just as I am, without one plea,
but that thy blood was shed for me,
and that thou bidd'st me come to thee,
O Lamb of God, I come, I come.

2 Just as I am, and waiting not
to rid my soul of one dark blot,
to thee, whose blood can cleanse each spot,
O Lamb of God, I come, I come.

3 Just as I am, though tossed about
with many a conflict, many a doubt,
fightings and fears within, without,
O Lamb of God, I come, I come.

4 Just as I am, thou wilt receive,
wilt welcome, pardon, cleanse, relieve;
because thy promise I believe:
O Lamb of God, I come, I come.

Poet: Charlotte Elliott, 1835. Meter: 8 8 8 8 (Long Meter).

Charlotte Elliott suffered from long-term physical impairments and mental anxiety ("...with many a conflict, many a doubt, fightings and fears within, without..."). Her experience of these conditions gave passion to her description of a Christian needing to come to God "Just as I am..." This hymn is often associated with the invitation or "altar call" at the conclusion of an evangelistic meeting, but it is very appropriate as a hymn of invitation to the Lord's Supper to which we all must come just as we are, admitting our need for God.

1 Jesus, the sinner's friend, to thee,
lost and undone, for aid I flee,
weary of earth, myself, and sin;
open thine arms, and take me in.

2 Pity and heal my sin-sick soul;
'tis thou alone canst make me whole;
dark, till in me thine image shine,
and lost, I am, till thou art mine.

3 At last I own it cannot be
that I should fit myself for thee.
Here, then, to thee I all resign;
thine is the work, and only thine.

4 What shall I say thy grace to move?
Lord, I am sin, but thou art love:
I give up every plea beside:
"Lord, I am lost, but thou hast died."

Poet: Charles Wesley, 1760. Meter: 8 8 8 8 (Long Meter).

Jesus said, "I have called you friends" (St John 15:15). Charles Wesley constantly called upon those who thought of themselves as sinners to realize that they are also Jesus' friends. Preparing grace is for all.

1 I heard the voice of Jesus say,
"Come unto me and rest;
lay down, thou weary one, lay down
thy head upon my breast."
I came to Jesus as I was,
so weary, worn, and sad;
I found in him a resting place,
and he has made me glad.

2 I heard the voice of Jesus say,
"Behold, I freely give
the living water, thirsty one;
stoop down, and drink, and live."
I came to Jesus, and I drank
of that life-giving stream;
my thirst was quenched, my soul revived,
and now I live in him.

3 I heard the voice of Jesus say,
"I am this dark world's Light;
look unto me, thy morn shall rise,
and all thy day be bright."
I looked to Jesus, and I found
in him my Star, my Sun;
and in that Light of life I'll walk,
till traveling days are done.

Poet: Horatius Bonar, 1846. Meter: 8 6 8 6 (Common Meter) doubled.

Another hymn of preparing grace, inviting sinners to find rest in Christ.
Notice how the poet envisions the bodily motion of humility: "stoop
down, and drink, and live."

1 Pass me not, O gentle Savior,
hear my humble cry;
while on others thou art calling,
do not pass me by.

Refrain:
Savior, Savior,
Hear my humble cry;
While on others Thou art calling,
do not pass me by.

2 Let me at a throne of mercy
find a sweet relief;
kneeling there in deep contrition,
help my unbelief. [Refrain]

3 Trusting only in thy merit,
would I seek thy face;
heal my wounded, broken spirit,
save me by thy grace. [Refrain]

4 Thou the Spring of all my comfort,
more than life to me;
whom have I on earth beside thee?
Whom in heaven but thee? [Refrain]

Poet: Frances Jane *née* Crosby Van Alstyne, 1868. Meter: 8 5 8 5 with refrain.

"Fanny Crosby," as she most often styled herself, imagines the cry of a repentant sinner to Jesus. Perhaps she was thinking about Zacchaeus (St Luke 19:1-10). The repentant person begs Jesus, "Do not pass me by!" That's how we as repentant sinners come to Jesus: "Hear my humble cry!"

1 Blow ye the trumpet, blow!
The gladly solemn sound.
Let all the nations know,
to earth's remotest bound:

Refrain:
The year of jubilee is come!
The year of jubilee is come!
Return, ye ransomed sinners, home.

2 Jesus, our great High Priest,
has full atonement made;
ye weary spirits, rest;
ye mournful souls, be glad: [Refrain]

3 Extol the Lamb of God,
the sacrificial Lamb;
redemption thro' his blood
throughout the world proclaim: [Refrain]

4 Ye slaves of sin and hell,
your liberty receive;
and safe in Jesus dwell,
and blest in Jesus live: [Refrain]

5 Ye who have sold for naught
your heritage above,
receive it back unbought,
the gift of Jesus' love: [Refrain]

6 The gospel trumpet hear,
the news of heavenly grace;
and, saved from earth, appear
before your Savior's face: [Refrain]

Poet: Charles Wesley, 1750. Meter: 6 6 6 6 with refrain added later.

This hymn utilizes the biblical image of the "year of jubilee" every 49th year when lands were to be returned to their original families. Whom does Charles Wesley invite to hear God's trumpet call? "Ye slaves of sin and hell"! Of course!

1 Depth of mercy! Can there be
mercy still reserved for me?
Can my God his wrath forbear?
me, the chief of sinners, spare?

2 I have long withstood his grace,
long provoked him to his face;
would not hearken to his calls,
grieved him by a thousand falls.

3 I my Master have denied;
I afresh have crucified,
oft profaned his hallowed name,
put him to an open shame.

4 There for me the Savior stands,
shows his wounds and spreads his hands.
God is love! I know, I feel;
Jesus weeps and loves me still!

5 Now incline me to repent,
let me now my fall lament;
now my foul revolt deplore!
weep, believe, and sin no more.

Poet: Charles Wesley, 1740. Meter: 7 7 7 7.

In this hymn of preparing grace, Charles Wesley empathizes with the
penitent soul who fears God's judgment: "Can there be mercy still reserved for me?" Even for "the chief of sinners"? The answer: "God is
love! I know, I feel; Jesus weeps and loves me still!"

1 Come, ye sinners, poor and needy,
weak and wounded, sick and sore;
Jesus ready stands to save you,
full of pity, love, and power.

> [Refrain:]
> I will arise and go to Jesus;
> he will embrace me in his arms;
> in the arms of my dear Savior,
> O there are ten thousand charms.

2 Come, ye thirsty, come, and welcome,
God's free bounty glorify;
true belief and true repentance,
every grace that brings you nigh. [Refrain]

3 Come, ye weary, heavy laden,
lost and ruined by the fall;
if you tarry 'til you're better,
you will never come at all. [Refrain]

4 Let not conscience make you linger,
nor of fitness fondly dream;
all the fitness he requireth
is to feel your need of him. [Refrain]

Poet: Joseph Hart, 1759. Meter: 8 7 8 7 with refrain.

Another hymn of preparing grace addressed to "sinners." Like Charles Wesley, Joseph Hart emphasizes Christ's compassion for those who feel excluded from God and perhaps from Christian communities. In the end, the only thing the sinner needs "is to feel your need of him."

## 63 Sinners, Turn: Why Will Ye Die?

1 Sinners, turn: why will ye die?
God, your maker, asks you why.
God, who did your being give,
made you with himself to live.

2 Sinners, turn: why will ye die?
God, your Savior, asks you why;
Will ye not in him believe?
He has died that ye might live.

3 Will you let him die in vain?
Crucify your Lord again?
Why, ye ransomed sinners, why
will you slight his grace and die?

4 Sinners, turn: why will ye die?
God, the Spirit, asks you why;
often with you has he strove,
wooed you to embrace his love.

5 Will ye not his grace receive?
Will ye still refuse to live?
O ye dying sinners, why,
why will you forever die?

Poet: Charles Wesley, 1742. Meter: 7 7 7 7.

Sinners, sinners, and more sinners! Woohoo! They're the peeps for whom these hymns of preparing grace are designed. These hymns don't call them to the great goal of complete or entire sanctification, just to the next step along the way: to recognize who they are and despite who they may be, to recognize God's love and call to them.

1 When all thy mercies, O my God,
my rising soul surveys,
transported with the view, I'm lost
in wonder, love, and praise.

2 Unnumbered comforts to my soul
thy tender care bestowed,
before my infant heart conceived
from whom those comforts flowed.

3 When in the slippery paths of youth
with heedless steps I ran,
thine arm unseen conveyed me safe,
and led me up to man.

4 Ten thousand thousand precious gifts
my daily thanks employ,
and not the least a cheerful heart
which tastes those gifts with joy.

5 Through every period of my life
thy goodness I'll pursue,
and after death in distant worlds
the glorious theme renew.

6 Through all eternity to thee,
a joyful song I'll raise;
for O, eternity's too short
to utter all thy praise.

Poet: Joseph Addison, 1712. Meter: 8 6 8 6 (Common Meter).

It's clear from this 1712 poem that Charles Wesley didn't make up the words "lost in wonder, love and praise" that he borrowed in "Love Divine! All Loves Excelling." This is a poem of simple recognition of all the good that God does for us.

## 65 Come, O Thou Traveler Unknown

1 Come, O thou traveler unknown,
whom still I hold, but cannot see!
My company before is gone,
and I am left alone with thee.
With thee all night I mean to stay
and wrestle till the break of day.

2 Wilt thou not yet to me reveal
thy new, unutterable name?
Tell me, I still beseech thee, tell,
to know it now resolved I am.
Wrestling, I will not let thee go
till I thy name, thy nature know.

3 My strength is gone, my nature dies,
I sink beneath thy weighty hand,
faint to revive, and fall to rise.
I fall, and yet by faith I stand;
I stand and will not let thee go
till I thy name, thy nature know.

4 Yield to me now—for I am weak,
but confident in self-despair!
Speak to my heart, in blessing speak,
be conquered by my instant prayer.
Speak, or thou never hence shalt move,
and tell me if thy name is LOVE.

5 'Tis LOVE! 'tis Love that wrestled me!
I hear thy whisper in my heart.
The morning breaks, the shadows flee,
PURE, UNIVERSAL LOVE thou art.
To me, to all, thy mercies move—
thy nature and thy name is LOVE.

Poet: Charles Wesley, 1742. Meter: 8 8 8 8 (Long Meter) doubled.

Charles Wesley's poetic masterpiece, originally 14 stanzas, uses the story of Jacob wrestling the mysterious stranger at Peniel (Genesis 32:24-32) to describe the revelation that God's true four-letter name is LOVE.

## The Way of Salvation: Justifying Grace

The second part of the Wesleys' teaching about "the way of salvation" was justification: the point at which through faith in Christ our past sins are forgiven. Justifying grace follows preparing grace: in fact, preparing grace is grace preparing people for justification.

The Wesleys both emphasized the personal experience or feeling—the feeling of *assurance* from God—that our sins have been forgiven. John and Charles Wesley could speak and write as if those who have not (yet) experienced this blessed assurance were not yet true believers. John Wesley eventually admitted that there were "exempt cases" in which people truly trusted in Christ but were not given the supernatural and personal assurance of justification.

1 And can it be that I should gain
an interest in the Savior's blood?
Died he for me, who caused his pain?
For me, who him to death pursued?
Amazing love! how can it be
that thou, my God, shouldst die for me?

2 'Tis mystery all! The immortal dies!
Who can explore his strange design?
In vain the firstborn seraph tries
to sound the depths of love divine!
'Tis mercy all! let earth adore,
let angel minds inquire no more.

3 He left his Father's throne above,
so free, so infinite his grace;
emptied himself of all but love,
and bled for Adam's helpless race;
'Tis mercy all, immense and free;
For O, my God, it found out me.

4 Long my imprisoned spirit lay
fast bound in sin and nature's night.
Thine eye diffused a quickening ray,
I woke, the dungeon flamed with light.
My chains fell off, my heart was free;
I rose, went forth and followed thee.

5 No condemnation now I dread;
Jesus, and all in him is mine!
Alive in him, my living head,
and clothed in righteousness divine,
bold I approach the eternal throne
and claim the crown, through Christ my own.

Poet: Charles Wesley, 1739. Meter: 8 8 8 8 8 8.

The expression "The immortal dies!" illustrates Charles Wesley's use of a contradiction to illustrate the mystery of the incarnation: "immortal" literally means "undying." How could "the immortal" die?

1 Come, thou fount of every blessing;
tune my heart to sing thy grace.
Streams of mercy, never ceasing,
call for songs of loudest praise.
Teach me some melodious sonnet,
sung by flaming tongues above.
Praise the mount! I'm fixed upon it,
mount of thy redeeming love!

2 Here I raise mine Ebenezer,
hither by thy help I'm come;
and I hope, by thy good pleasure,
safely to arrive at home.
Jesus sought me when a stranger,
wandering from the fold of God;
he, to rescue me from danger,
interposed his precious blood.

3 O to grace how great a debtor
daily I'm constrained to be!
Let thy goodness, like a fetter,
bind my wandering heart to thee.
Prone to wander, Lord, I feel it,
prone to leave the God I love;
here's my heart; O take and seal it;
seal it for thy courts above.

Poet: Robert Robinson, 1758. Meter: 8 7 8 7 doubled.

"Ebenezer": a Biblical image of a memorial to victory. Ebenezer (He-brew: *eben-ezer*) means "the stone of help." I Samuel 7:2-14 describes Samuel erecting a stone to remember the Israelites' victory over Phil-istines at Ebenezer.

The word "stranger" here ("Jesus sought me when a stranger...") car-ries the meaning of "alien" or "foreigner." But Christ brings us into his radically inclusive fellowship: "So then you are no longer strangers and aliens, but you are citizens with the saints and also members of the household of God" (Ephesians 2:19).

1 How can we sinners know
our sins on earth forgiven?
How can my gracious Savior show
my name inscribed in heaven?

2 What we have felt and seen
with confidence we tell,
and publish to the ends of earth
the signs infallible.

3 We who in Christ believe
that he for us hath died,
we all his unknown peace receive,
and feel his blood applied.

4 We by his Spirit prove
and know the things of God,
the things which freely of his love
he hath on us bestowed.

5 The meek and lowly heart
that in our Savior was:
to use that Spirit doth impart
and signs us with his cross.

6 Our nature's turned, our mind
transformed in all its powers,
and both the witnesses are joined,
the Spirit of God with ours.

Charles Wesley, 1749. Meter: 6 6 8 6 (Short Meter).

This hymn teaches the Wesleyan doctrine of the twofold assurance of
justification: the "inward witness" of God's own Spirit assuring us our
sins are forgiven, and the "outward witness" of the change of our own
spirits by grace, so that "both the witnesses are joined, the Spirit of God
with ours."

1 Blessed assurance, Jesus is mine!
Oh, what a foretaste of glory divine!
Heir of salvation, purchase of God,
born of his Spirit, washed in his blood.

> Refrain:
> This is my story, this is my song,
> praising my Savior all the day long.
> This is my story, this is my song,
> praising my Savior all the day long.

2 Perfect submission, perfect delight,
visions of rapture now burst on my sight.
Angels descending bring from above
echoes of mercy, whispers of love. [Refrain]

3 Perfect submission, all is at rest.
I in my Savior am happy and blessed,
watching and waiting, looking above,
filled with his goodness, lost in his love. [Refrain]

Poet: Frances Jane *née* Crosby Van Alstyne, 1873. Meter: 9 10 9 9 with refrain.

The blind Methodist poet who most often styled herself "Fanny Crosby" offers her own understanding of the historic Wesleyan doctrine of the assurance of our forgiveness by God. Charles Wesley had written a poem on or just after the day of his conversion experience in which he called this assurance an "antepast" (a foretaste) of heaven (see *United Methodist Hymnal* 1989, no. 342). Fanny Crosby understands the experience of divine forgiveness similarly as "a foretaste of glory divine."

1 Spirit of faith, come down,
Reveal the things of God;
And make to us the Godhead known,
And witness with the blood.
'Tis Thine the blood to apply,
And give us eyes to see,
Who did for every sinner die,
Hath surely died for me.

2 No one can truly say
That Jesus is the Lord,
Unless thou take the veil away,
And breathe the living word.
Then, only then, we feel
Our interest in His blood,
And cry, with joy unspeakable,
"Thou art my Lord, my God!"

3 O that the world might know
The all-atoning Lamb!
Spirit of faith, descend, and show
The virtue of His name.
The grace which all may find,
The saving power, impart;
And testify to all mankind,
And speak in every heart.

Poet: Charles Wesley, 1746. Meter: 6 6 8 6 (Short Meter) doubled.

Like the previous hymn, this hymn reflects the early Methodist teaching about assurance that a person can have a direct, personal knowledge given by God that their sins have been forgiven through faith in Christ. The second verse suggests that no human can confess that "Jesus is Lord" without the work of the Spirit. John Wesley allowed that there might be "exempt cases in which a person truly believed but did not feel a supernatural assurance of forgiveness. Discussion of personal religious experiences has been a consistent part of Methodist culture.

1 O happy day that fixed my choice
on Thee, my Savior and my God!
Well may this glowing heart rejoice,
and tell its raptures all abroad.

Refrain:
Happy day! Happy day!
When Jesus washed my sins away!
He taught me how to watch and pray,
And live rejoicing every day:
Happy day! Happy day!
When Jesus washed my sins away!

2 O happy bond, that seals my vows
to Him who merits all my love!
Let cheerful anthems fill His house,
while to that sacred shrine I move. [Refrain]

3 'Tis done, the great transaction's done;
I am my Lord's and He is mine.
He drew me and I followed on,
rejoiced to own the call divine. [Refrain]

4 Now rest, my long-divided heart,
fixed on this blissful center, rest.
Here have I found a nobler part,
here heavenly pleasures fill my breast. [Refrain]

5 High heaven that hears the solemn vow,
that vow renewed shall daily hear;
till in life's latest hour I bow,
and bless, in death, a bond so dear. [Refrain]

Poet: Phillip Doddridge, 1755. The refrain is from the *Wesleyan Sacred Harp*, 1854. Meter: 8 8 6 8 with refrain added later.

This hymn reflects the belief that our sins are forgiven by faith in Christ that involves a *choice* to trust in Christ. But this choice is not a human work: it is itself the work of God's preparatory (or "prevenient") grace.

1 Arise, my soul, arise, shake off thy guilty fears:
the bleeding sacrifice in my behalf appears.
Before the throne my surety stands,
before the throne my surety stands:
my name is written on his hands.

2 He ever lives above for me to intercede:
his all-redeeming love, his precious blood to plead.
His blood atoned for all our race,
his blood atoned for all our race,
and sprinkles now the throne of grace.

3 Five bleeding wounds he bears, received on Calvary:
they pour effectual prayers, they strongly plead for me.
"Forgive him, O, forgive," they cry,
"Forgive him, O, forgive," they cry,
"Nor let that ransomed sinner die!"

4 The Father hears him pray, his dear Anointed One;
he cannot turn away the presence of his Son.
His Spirit answers to the blood,
his Spirit answers to the blood,
and tells me I am born of God.

5 My God is reconciled, his pardoning voice I hear;
he owns me for a child; I can no longer fear.
With confidence I now draw nigh,
with confidence I now draw nigh,
and, "Father, Abba, Father," cry.

Poet: Charles Wesley, 1742. Meter: 6 6 6 6 8 8 8.

The image of Christ's wounds crying out on behalf of sinner may bewilder or even offend contemporary folks. The Wesleys followed a long tradition of medieval Catholic devotion that celebrated the wounds of Christ and often envisioned them speaking on behalf of sinners.

1 Jesus, thy blood and righteousness
my beauty are, my glorious dress;
'midst flaming worlds, in these arrayed,
with joy shall I lift up my head.

2 Bold shall I stand in thy great day,
for who aught to my charge shall lay?
Fully absolved through these I am,
from sin and fear, from guilt and shame.

3 Lord, I believe thy precious blood,
which at the mercy seat of God,
forever doth for sinners plead,
for me, e'en for my soul, was shed.

4 Jesus, be endless praise to thee,
whose boundless mercy hath for me,
for me a full atonement made,
an everlasting ransom paid.

5 When from the dust of death I rise
to claim my mansion in the skies,
e'en then this shall be all my plea,
Jesus hath lived, hath died, for me.

6 O let the dead now hear thy voice;
now bid thy ransomed ones rejoice;
their beauty this, their glorious dress,
Jesus, thy blood and righteousness.

Poet: Nicolas Ludwig, Graf [Count] von Zinzendorf; translated by John
Wesley, 1739. Meter: 8 8 8 8 (Long Meter).

Zinzendorf was the leader of the reconstituted Moravian community
that had fled from Central Europe and were given refuge at Zinzendorf's estate Herrnhut. He and John Wesley differed strongly over their
teachings about sanctifying grace (see the next section), but they con-
curred in the teaching expressed here about Christ's righteousness as
the grounds of our salvation.

1 From every stormy wind that blows,
from every swelling tide of woes,
there is a calm, a sure retreat:
'tis found beneath the mercy seat.

2 There is a place where Jesus sheds
the oil of gladness on our heads;
a place than all beside more sweet:
it is the blood-bought mercy seat.

3 There is a scene where spirits blend,
where friend holds fellowship with friend;
though sundered far, by faith they meet
around one common mercy seat.

4 Ah! there on eagle wings we soar,
where sin and sense molest no more;
and heaven comes down our souls to greet,
and glory crowns the mercy seat.

Poet: Hugh Stowell, 1828. Meter: 8 8 8 8 (Long Meter).

The "mercy seat" was the lid for the Ark of the Covenant in the Israelite Tabernacle and the Jewish Temple in Jerusalem, the place where sacrificial offerings were made. Christians came to understand Christ's incarnation and life and death and resurrection together as his one offering to God for the sins of the whole world. So the "mercy seat" is for Christians an indication of Christ's self-outpouring on our behalf.

1 Rock of Ages, cleft for me,
let me hide myself in thee;
let the water and the blood,
from thy wounded side which flowed,
be of sin the double cure;
save from wrath and make me pure.

2 Not the labors of my hands
can fulfill thy law's demands;
could my zeal no respite know,
could my tears forever flow,
all for sin could not atone;
thou must save, and thou alone.

3 Nothing in my hand I bring,
simply to the cross I cling;
naked, come to thee for dress;
helpless, look to thee for grace;
foul, I to the fountain fly;
wash me, Savior, or I die.

4 While I draw this fleeting breath,
when mine eyes shall close in death,
when I soar to worlds unknown,
see thee on thy judgment throne,
Rock of Ages, cleft for me,
let me hide myself in thee.

Poet: Augustus M. Toplady, 1776. Meter: 7 7 7 7 7 7.

Augustus Toplady was known to be a strongly Calvinist and even anti-Wesleyan writer. He may have designed "Rock of Ages" as an attack on what he perceived to be an arrogant Wesleyan over-emphasis on good works following justification: "Nothing in my hand I bring / only to thy cross I cling…" But Wesleyans were more inclined to plead for divine grace than Toplady may have imagined, and they consistently included "Rock of Ages" in Methodist hymn collections.

1 My faith looks up to thee,
thou Lamb of Calvary,
Savior divine!
Now hear me while I pray,
take all my guilt away;
O let me from this day
be wholly thine.

2 May thy rich grace impart
strength to my fainting heart,
my zeal inspire;
as thou hast died for me,
O may my love to thee
pure, warm, and changeless be,
a living fire.

3 While life's dark maze I tread,
and griefs around me spread,
be thou my guide;
bid darkness turn to day,
wipe sorrow's tears away,
nor let me ever stray
from thee aside.

4 When ends life's transient dream,
when death's cold, sullen stream
shall o'er me roll,
blest Savior, then in love,
fear and distrust remove;
O bear me safe above,
a ransomed soul.

Poet: Ray Palmer, 1830. Meter: 664.6664.

Homer Thrall's *History of Methodism in Texas* (1872) describes an traveling preacher thrown from his horse while crossing a flooded river. He thought he was dying and recalled the words of this hymn: "...when death's cold, sullen stream shall o'er me roll..." Then he felt something brushy: it was his horse's tail and he hung on as the horse dragged him to shore (page 72).

1 O Love divine, that stooped to share
our sharpest pang, our bitterest tear!
On Thee we cast each earth-born care;
we smile at pain while thou art near.

2 Though long the weary way we tread,
and sorrow crown each lingering year,
no path we shun, no darkness dread,
our hearts still whispering, "Thou art near!"

3 When drooping pleasure turns to grief,
and trembling faith is turned to fear,
the murmuring wind, the quivering leaf,
shall softly tell us thou art near!

4 On thee we fling our burdening woe,
O Love divine, for ever dear!
Content to suffer, while we know,
living and dying, thou art near!

Poet: Oliver Wendell Holmes, 1859. Meter: 8 8 8 8 (Long Meter).

The word "stoop" recalled the common posture of kneeling to pray, and
we have seen it above in hymns calling for repentance. But in Justice
Holmes's hymn, it is God's own love that "stooped to share" our griefs
and fears.

1 There is a fountain filled with blood
Drawn from Immanuel's veins;
And sinners, plunged beneath that flood,
lose all their guilty stains. (x3)
And sinners, plunged beneath that flood,
lose all their guilty stains.

2 The dying thief rejoiced to see
that fountain in his day;
and there may I, though vile as he,
wash all my sins away: (x3)
And there may I, though vile as he,
wash all my sins away.

3 Dear dying Lamb, thy precious blood
shall never lose its power,
till all the ransomed Church of God
be saved to sin no more. (x3)
Till all the ransomed Church of God
be saved to sin no more.

4 E'er since by faith I saw the stream
thy flowing wounds supply,
redeeming love has been my theme,
and shall be till I die: (x3)
Redeeming love has been my theme,
and shall be till I die.

5 When this poor lisping, stammering tongue
lies silent in the grave,
then in a nobler, sweeter song
I'll sing thy power to save. (x3)
Then in a nobler, sweeter song
I'll sing thy power to save.

Poet: William Cowper, 1772 (Zechariah 13:1). Meter: 8 6 8 6 (Common Meter) doubled.

Cowper's hymn is an early example of what came to be called the "blood hymns" by squeamish Protestants. But it is about Christ's sacrificial self-giving work for all human beings.

1 O thou to whose all-searching sight
the darkness shineth as the light,
search, prove my heart, it pants for thee;
O burst these bonds and set it free!

2 Wash out its stain, refine its dross,
nail my affections to the cross:
hallow each thought, let all within
be clean, as thou, my Lord, art clean.

3 Savior, where'er thy steps I see,
dauntless, untired, I'll follow thee;
O let thy hand support me still
and lead me to thy holy hill!

4 If rough and thorny be the way,
my strength proportion to my day,
till toil and grief and pain shall cease,
where all is calm and joy and peace.

Poet: Nicolaus Ludwig, Graf von Zinzendorf; translated by John Wesley, 1721. Meter: 8 8 8 8 (Long Meter).

Another hymn by the Moravian reorganizer Zinzendorf calling for reliance on God's grace in challenging times and situations.

## The Way of Salvation: Sanctifying Grace

The third part of the Wesleyan and Methodist understanding of the "way of salvation" is sanctifying grace: God's grace leading us to greater and greater holiness. The goal Methodists have envisioned is entire sanctification: complete love for God and neighbor as a gift of divine grace. It is the fulfillment of the Great Commandment: "You shall love the Lord your God with all your heart, and with all your soul, and with all your understanding, and with all your strength" (St Mark 12:30). Methodist hymnals typically have more hymns in their sections on sanctifying grace than in any other section and that is also true of this *Core Methodist Hymnal.*

1 Love divine, all loves excelling,
joy of heaven to earth come down,
fix in us thy humble dwelling;
all thy faithful mercies crown!
Jesus, thou art all compassion,
pure, unbounded love thou art;
visit us with thy salvation;
enter every trembling heart.

2 Breathe, O breathe thy loving Spirit
into every troubled breast!
Let us all in thee inherit,
let us find that second rest.
Take away our bent to sinning;
Alpha and Omega be;
end of faith, as its beginning,
set our hearts at liberty.

3 Come, Almighty to deliver;
let us all thy life receive;
suddenly return and never,
never more thy temples leave.
Thee we would be always blessing,
serve thee as thy hosts above;
pray, and praise thee without ceasing,
glory in thy perfect love.

4 Finish then, thy new creation;
pure and spotless let us be;
let us see thy great salvation
perfectly restored in thee.
Changed from glory into glory,
till in heaven we take our place,
till we cast our crowns before thee,
lost in wonder, love, and praise.

Poet: Charles Wesley, 1747. Meter: 8 7 8 7 doubled.

This is Charles Wesley's masterpiece hymn of entire sanctification or
"Christian perfection," complete love for God and neighbor.

1 O thou who camest from above
the pure celestial fire to impart:
kindle a flame of sacred love
on the mean altar of my heart!

2 There let it for thy glory burn
with inextinguishable blaze,
and trembling to its source return
in humble prayer and fervent praise.

3 Jesus, confirm my heart's desire
to work, and speak, and think for thee;
still let me guard the holy fire,
and still stir up the gift in me.

4 Ready for all thy perfect will,
my acts of faith and love repeat;
till death thy endless mercies seal,
and make the sacrifice complete.

Poet: Charles Wesley, 1762. Meter:  8 8 8 8 (Long Meter).

Christ's outpouring of love calls for the reciprocal outpouring of our
own love for God and others. Charles Wesley calls down the Holy Spirit
to kindle the fire of God's love, God's grace, in us.

1 Jesus, thy boundless love to me,
no thought can reach, no tongue declare.
O knit my thankful heart to thee
and reign without a rival there.
Thine wholly, thine alone, I am;
be thou my rod and staff and guide.

2 O grant that nothing in my soul
may dwell, but thy pure love alone!
O may thy love possess my whole,
my joy, my treasure, and my crown.
All coldness from my heart remove;
my every act, word, thought, be love.

3 O love, how cheering is thy ray!
All pain before thy presence flies;
care, anguish, sorrow, melt away,
where'er thy healing beams arise.
O Jesus, nothing may I see,
nothing desire or seek, but thee.

4 This love unwearied I pursue
and dauntlessly to thee aspire.
O may thy love my hope renew,
burn in my soul like heav'nly fire.
And day and night, be all my care
to guard this sacred treasure there.

Poet: Paul Gerhardt, 1653; translated into English by John Wesley, 1739. Meter: 8 8 8 8 8 8.

A prayer from the Lutheran hymn writer Paul Gerhardt in the seventeenth century asking that the fire of Jesus' love would "possess my whole," the entirety of who we are, enabling us to return God's love and share it with others. That's what Methodists mean by "entire sanctification,"

1 How sweet the name of Jesus sounds
in a believer's ear!
It soothes our sorrows, heals our wounds,
and drives away our fear.

2 It makes the wounded spirit whole
and calms the troubled breast;
'tis manna to the hungry soul,
and to the weary, rest.

3 Jesus, my Savior, shepherd, friend,
my prophet, priest, and king,
my Lord, my life, my way, my end,
accept the praise I bring.

4 Weak is the effort of my heart,
and cold my warmest thought;
but when I see thee as thou art,
I'll praise thee as I ought.

5 Till then I would thy love proclaim
with every fleeting breath;
and may the music of thy name
refresh my soul in death.

Poet: John Newton, 1779 (Song of Solomon 1:3). Meter: 8686 (Common Meter).

Another hymn from Newton's and Cowper's *Olney Hymns* (1779) invoking the sacred name of Jesus to empower us in life and in death.

1 Nothing between my soul and the Savior,
naught of this world's delusive dream:
I have renounced all sinful pleasure-
Jesus is mine! There's nothing between.

> Refrain:
> Nothing between my soul and the Savior,
> so that His blessed face may be seen;
> nothing preventing the least of His favor:
> Keep the way clear! Let nothing between.

2 Nothing between, like worldly pleasure:
habits of life, though harmless they seem,
must not my heart from him ever sever:
he is my all! There's nothing between. [Refrain]

3 Nothing between, like pride or station:
self or friends shall not intervene;
though it may cost me much tribulation:
I am resolved! There's nothing between. [Refrain]

4 Nothing between, e'en many hard trials,
though the whole world against me convene;
watching with prayer and much self denial:
Triumph at last, with nothing between! [Refrain]

Poet: Charles Albert Tindley, ca. 1906. Meter: 10 9 11 9 with refrain.

Charles Albert Tindley was the pastor of a multi-racial Philadelphia Methodist congregation now called Tindley Temple. Here he celebrates the goal of sanctification as complete love for God, a relationship in which there is, in his vision, "nothing between my soul and the Savior"!

1 O love divine, how sweet thou art!
When shall I find my longing heart
all taken up by thee?
I thirst, I faint, I die to prove
the greatness of redeeming love,
the love of Christ to me.

2 Stronger his love than death or hell;
its riches are unsearchable:
the first-born sons of light
desire in vain its depth to see;
they cannot reach the mystery,
the length and breadth and height.

3 God only knows the love of God;
O that it now were shed abroad
in this poor stony heart!
For love I sigh, for love I pine;
this only portion, Lord, be mine,
be mine this better part.

4 For ever would I take my seat
with Mary at the Master's feet:
be this my happy choice;
my only care, delight, and bliss,
my joy, my heaven on earth, be this,
to hear the Bridegroom's voice!

5 Thy only love do I require,
nothing on earth beneath desire,
nothing in heaven above:
let earth and heaven, and all things go,
give me thine only love to know,
give me thine only love.

Poet: Charles Wesley, 1749. Meter: 8 8 6 8 8 6.

This is another Charles Wesley hymn about entire sanctification: "When
shall I find my longing heart all taken up by thee?" Entire sanctification is
when our hearts are indeed "all taken up" with God.

1 Children of the heavenly King,
as we journey let us sing;
sing our Savior's worthy praise,
glorious in his works and ways.

2 We are traveling home to God,
in the way our fathers trod;
they are happy now, and we
soon their happiness shall see.

3 Fear not, brethren; joyful stand
on the borders of our land;
Jesus Christ, our Father's Son,
bids us undismayed go on.

4 Lord, obediently we'll go,
gladly leaving all below;
only thou our leader be,
and we still will follow thee.

Poet: John Cennick, 1743. Meter: 7 7 7 7.

Moravian minister John Cennick offers a pilgrim hymn, envisioning the
path to sanctification as a journey: "We are traveling home to God."

1 O for a closer walk with God,
a calm and heav'nly frame,
a light to shine upon the road
that leads me to the Lamb!

2 Where is the blessedness I knew
when first I sought the Lord?
Where is the soul refreshing view
of Jesus and his Word?

3 What peaceful hours I then enjoyed!
How sweet their mem'ry still!
But they have left an aching void
the world can never fill.

4 Return, O holy dove, return,
sweet messenger of rest;
I hate the sins that made thee mourn,
and drove thee from my breast.

5 The dearest idol I have known,
whate'er that idol be,
help me to tear it from thy throne
and worship only thee.

6 So shall my walk be close with God,
calm and serene my frame;
so purer light shall mark the road
that leads me to the Lamb.

Poet: William Cowper, 1772. Meter: 8 6 8 6 (Common Meter).

Like the previous hymn by Cennick, Cowper also envisioned the path
to sanctification as a pilgrimage, a journey of the soul. Cowper envisions that the soul might lose its way and leave "an aching void the
world can never fill..." But he prays to return to the good path and continue the journey.

1 What a friend we have in Jesus,
all our sins and griefs to bear!
What a privilege to carry
everything to God in prayer!
O what peace we often forfeit,
O what needless pain we bear,
all because we do not carry
everything to God in prayer!

2 Have we trials and temptations?
Is there trouble anywhere?
We should never be discouraged;
take it to the Lord in prayer!
Can we find a friend so faithful
who will all our sorrows share?
Jesus knows our every weakness;
take it to the Lord in prayer!

3 Are we weak and heavy laden,
cumbered with a load of care?
Precious Savior, still our refuge:
take it to the Lord in prayer!
Do your friends despise, forsake thee?
Take it to the Lord in prayer!
In his arms he'll take and shield thee;
thou will find a solace there.

Poet: Joseph M. Scriven, ca. 1855. Meter: 8 7 8 7 doubled.

Part of the process of sanctification is dealing with the challenges we face along the way to complete holiness (entire sanctification). Joseph M. Scriven advises us in this hymn to "Take it to the Lord in Prayer" whenever we face problems.

1 He leadeth me: O blessed thought!
O words with heavenly comfort fraught!
Whate'er I do, where'er I be,
still 'tis God's hand that leadeth me.

> Refrain:
> He leadeth me, he leadeth me;
> by his own hand he leadeth me:
> his faithful follower I would be,
> for by his hand he leadeth me.

2 Sometimes mid scenes of deepest gloom,
sometimes where Eden's flowers bloom,
by waters calm, o'er troubled sea,
still 'tis God's hand that leadeth me. [Refrain]

3 Lord, I would clasp thy hand in mine,
nor ever murmur nor repine;
content, whatever lot I see,
since 'tis my God that leadeth me. [Refrain]

4 And when my task on earth is done,
when, by thy grace, the victory's won,
e'en death's cold wave I will not flee,
since God through Jordan leadeth me. [Refrain]

Poet: Joseph Henry Gilmore, 1862. Meter: 8 8 8 8 (Long Meter) with refrain.

Another aspect of sanctification is learning to follow God's guidance. Joseph Henry Gilmore teaches us that through life and even as we approach death ("And when my task on earth is done…"), we must continually ask for God's guidance.

1 O for a heart to praise my God,
a heart from sin set free;
a heart that's sprinkled with the blood
so freely shed for me;

2 A heart resigned, submissive, meek,
my great Redeemer's throne;
where only Christ is heard to speak,
where Jesus reigns alone;

3 A humble, lowly, contrite heart,
believing, true, and clean,
which neither life nor death can part
from him that dwells within:

4 A heart in every thought renewed,
and full of love divine;
perfect and right and pure and good —
a copy, Lord, of thine.

5 Thy nature, gracious Lord, impart,
come quickly from above;
write thy new name upon my heart,
thy new best name of LOVE.

Poet: Charles Wesley, 1742. Meter: 8 6 8 6 (Common Meter).

Charles Wesley's hymns are a guide to sanctification. In this hymn, he leads us in praying for a heart that submits to God. I don't think he meant that we should become doormats to be trampled on: in others of his hymns, he prays for strength to resist evil and temptations. But God knows our needs, so we rely on God and God's power.

1 Father, I stretch my hands to thee,
no other help I know.
If thou withdraw thyself from me,
O whither shall I go?

2 What did thine only son endure,
before I drew my breath!
What pain, what labor to secure
my soul from endless death!

3 Surely thou canst not let me die;
O speak and I shall live.
And here I will unwearied lie,
till thou thy Spirit give.

4 Author of faith! to thee I lift
my weary, longing eyes.
O let me now receive that gift:
my soul without it dies.

Poet: Charles Wesley 1741. Meter: 8 6 8 6 (Common Meter).

Charles Wesley's hymn text "Father, I Stretch My Hands to Thee" is a favorite in historically Black churches in the United States. It is often sung with a precentor (a "pre-singer") lining out each line and then letting the congregation sing it back slowly with improvised harmony. This very moving style was described to me as "Singin' a Dr Watts Hymn": even if the author was Charles Wesley!

1 Jesus, lover of my soul,
let me to thy bosom fly,
while the nearer waters roll,
while the tempest still is high;
hide me, O my Savior, hide,
till the storm of life is past;
safe into the haven guide,
O receive my soul at last!

2 Other refuge have I none;
hangs my helpless soul on thee;
leave, ah! leave me not alone,
still support and comfort me.
All my trust on thee is stayed,
all my help from thee I bring;
cover my defenseless head
with the shadow of thy wing.

3 Plenteous grace with thee is found,
grace to cover all my sin;
let the healing streams abound;
make and keep me pure within.
Thou of life the fountain art;
freely let me take of thee;
spring thou up within my heart,
rise to all eternity.

Poet: Charles Wesley, 1740. Meter: 77 77 doubled.

An explosion in the Welsh mining town Aberfan in 1966 killed 116 children—most of them students at school—and 28 adults as well. When the community gathered to mourn their loss, they sang "Jesus, Lover of My Soul," in Welsh to the tune ABERYSTWYTH. The event including the impact of the hymn on the British royal family is depicted in the Netflix video series "The Crown."

1 Sometimes a light surprises
the Christian while he sings;
it is the Lord who rises
with healing in his wings.
When comforts are declining,
he grants the soul again
a season of clear shining,
to cheer it after rain.

2 In holy contemplation,
we sweetly then pursue
the theme of God's salvation,
and find it ever new.
Set free from present sorrow,
we cheerfully can say,
"E'en let the unknown morrow
bring with it what it may."

3 "It can bring with it nothing,
but he will bear us through;
who gives the lilies clothing
will clothe his people, too;
beneath the spreading heavens
no creature but is fed;
and he who feeds the ravens
will give his children bread."

4 Though vine nor fig tree neither
their wonted fruit should bear;
though all the field should wither
nor flocks nor herds be there;
yet God the same abiding,
his praise shall tune my voice;
for while in him confiding,
I cannot but rejoice.

Poet: William Cowper, 1779 (St Matthew 6:25-34; Habakkuk 3:17-18).
Meter: 7 6 7 6 doubled.

Cowper celebrates the sometimes-unexpected power of Christian music and poetry that lead us along the path to sanctification.

1 Sweet hour of prayer! sweet hour of prayer!
that calls me from a world of care,
and bids me at my Father's throne
make all my wants and wishes known.
In seasons of distress and grief,
my soul has often found relief,
and oft escaped the tempter's snare
by thy return, sweet hour of prayer!

2 Sweet hour of prayer! sweet hour of prayer!
the joys I feel, the bliss I share
of those whose anxious spirits burn
with strong desires for thy return!
With such I hasten to the place
where God my Savior shows his face,
and gladly take my station there,
and wait for thee, sweet hour of prayer!

3 Sweet hour of prayer! Sweet hour of prayer!
Thy wings shall my petition bear
to him whose truth and faithfulness
engage the waiting soul to bless.
And since he bids me seek his face,
believe his word, and trust his grace,
I'll cast on him my every care,
and wait for thee, sweet hour of prayer!

Poet: William Walford, 1845. Meter: 8 8 8 8 (Long Meter) doubled.

A homeless man asked me to help him get food. I did, and I asked him in return, "Can you tell me how to become holy?" He said, "Well, you better pray a lot!" He must have known I needed it. That's what William Walford's beloved hymn is about: regular prayer as a way to sanctification: "sweet hour of prayer"!

1 Talk with us, Lord, thyself reveal,
while here o'er earth we rove.
Speak to our hearts, and let us feel
the kindling of thy love.

2 With thee conversing, we forget
all time and toil and care;
labor is rest, and pain is sweet,
if thou, my God, art here.

3 Thou callest me to seek thy face,
'tis all I wish to seek;
to hear the whispers of thy grace,
and hear thee in me speak.

4 Let this my every hour employ,
till I thy glory see,
enter into my Master's joy,
and find my heaven in thee.

Poet: Charles Wesley, 1740. Meter: 8 6 8 6 (Common Meter).

Do you ever hear God speaking to you in prayer? I don't, and I think that's not fair. What does Charles Wesley mean when he says that God speaks to "our hearts"? Like you get funny feelings? I get funny feelings all the time, but I'm never sure they're from God. Help me! (That's a prayer.)

1 Prayer is the soul's sincere desire,
unuttered or expressed,
the motion of a hidden fire
that trembles in the breast.

2 Prayer is the burden of a sigh,
the falling of a tear,
the upward glancing of an eye
when none but God is near.

3 Prayer is the simplest form of speech
that infant lips can try,
prayer the sublimest strains that reach
the majesty on high.

4 Prayer is the contrite sinner's voice,
returning from their way,
while angels in their songs rejoice
and cry, "Behold, they pray!"

5 Prayer is the Christian's vital breath,
the Christian's native air,
his watchword at the gates of death:
he enters heaven with prayer.

6 O thou by whom we come to God,
the life, the truth, the way,
the path of prayer thyself hast trod:
Lord, teach us how to pray!

Poet: James Montgomery, 1818. Meter: 8 6 8 6 (Common Meter).

Once I actually read it, I realized that this is a really, really different kind of hymn. Does James Montgomery mean that any time a person—any person whatsoever—experiences a "sincere desire, unuttered or expressed," that's a prayer to God? Is prayer really "the simplest form of speech that infant lips can try"? Wow.

1 I need thee every hour,
most gracious Lord;
no tender voice like thine
can peace afford.

> Refrain:
> I need thee, O, I need thee;
> every hour I need thee;
> O, bless me now, my Savior,
> I come to thee.

2 I need thee every hour,
stay thou nearby.
Temptations lose their power
when thou art nigh. [Refrain]

3 I need thee every hour,
in joy or pain.
Come quickly and abide,
or life is vain. [Refrain]

4 I need thee every hour,
teach me thy will;
and thy rich promises
in me fulfill. [Refrain]

5 I need thee every hour,
O thou most holy one.
O make me thine indeed,
thou blessed Son. [Refrain]

Poet: Annie S. Hawks, 1872 (St John 15:5). Meter: 6 4 6 4 with refrain.

I can still hear my mother's alto voice on this one. It's a good thing for children to hear their parents sing that they need God every hour. But I may have been the reason.

1 Thou hidden source of calm repose,
thou all-sufficient love divine;
my help and refuge from my foes,
secure I am, if thou art mine.
And lo! from sin and grief and shame
I hide me, Jesus, in thy name.

2 Thy mighty name salvation is,
and keeps my happy soul above;
comfort it brings, and power and peace,
and joy and everlasting love;
to me, with thy dear name, are given
pardon and holiness and heaven.

3 Jesus, my all in all thou art;
my rest in toil, my ease in pain,
the healing of my broken heart,
in war my peace, in loss my gain,
my smile beneath the tyrant's frown,
in shame my glory and my crown.

4 In want my plentiful supply,
in weakness my almighty power,
in bonds my perfect liberty,
my light in Satan's darkest hour,
my help and stay whene'er I call,
my life in death, my heaven, my all.

Poet: Charles Wesley, 1749. Meter: 8 8 8 8 8 8.

ADHD people like me need "calm repose." Always fidgeting. "Calm repose" takes great concentration and singing a hymn helps even more
than listening to one or reading one. I think.

1 Thou hidden Love of God, whose height,
whose depth unfathomed, no man knows,
I see from far thy beauteous light,
and inly sigh for thy repose;
my heart is pained, nor can it be
at rest till it finds rest in thee.

2 'Tis mercy all that thou hast brought
my mind to seek its peace in thee;
yet while I seek, but find thee not,
no peace my wandering soul shall see.
O when shall all my wanderings end,
and all my steps to thee-ward tend?

3 Is there a thing beneath the sun
that strives with thee my heart to share?
Ah! tear it thence, and reign alone,
the Lord of every motion there;
then shall my heart from earth be free,
when it has found repose in thee.

4 O Love, thy sovereign aid impart
to save me from low-thoughted care;
chase this self-will from all my heart,
from all its hidden mazes there;
make me Thy duteous child, that I
may ceaseless "Abba, Father," cry.

5 Each moment draw from earth away
my heart, that lowly waits thy call;
speak to my inmost soul, and say
"I am thy Love, thy God, thy all."
To feel thy power, to hear thy voice,
to taste thy love, be all my choice!

Gerhard Tersteegen, 1729; translated by John Wesley. Meter: 8 8 8 8 8 8.

If you're reading through this hymnal, you'll realize by now that John Wesley translated several German hymn compositions like this one that subsequently came into Methodist hymnals.

1 How firm a foundation, ye saints of the Lord,
is laid for your faith in his excellent Word!
What more can he say than to you he hath said,
to you who for refuge to Jesus have fled?

2 "Fear not, I am with thee, O be not dismayed,
for I am thy God, and will still give thee aid;
I'll strengthen thee, help thee, and cause thee to stand,
upheld by my righteous, omnipotent hand.

3 "When through the deep waters I call thee to go,
the rivers of sorrow shall not overflow;
for I will be near thee, thy troubles to bless,
and sanctify to thee thy deepest distress.

4 "When through fiery trials thy pathway shall lie,
my grace, all sufficient, shall be thy supply;
the flame shall not hurt thee; I only design
thy dross to consume, and thy gold to refine.

5 "The soul that on Jesus hath leaned for repose,
I will not, I will not desert to its foes;
that soul, though all hell should endeavor to shake,
I'll never, no never, no never forsake."

Poet: Robert Keen (Isaiah 43:2), 1787. Meter: 11 11 11 11.

Robert Keen's poem is based on Isaiah 43:2: "When you pass through the waters, I will be with you; and through the rivers, they shall not overwhelm you; when you walk through fire you shall not be burned, and the flame shall not consume you." Isaiah and Keen's poem celebrate God's power to deliver us from the fates we fear.

1 I want a principle within
of watchful, godly fear,
a sensibility of sin,
a pain to feel it near.
I want the first approach to feel
of pride or wrong desire,
to catch the wandering of my will,
and quench the kindling fire.

2 From thee that I no more may stray,
no more thy goodness grieve,
grant me the filial awe, I pray,
the tender conscience, give.
Quick as the apple of an eye,
O God, my conscience make;
Awake my soul when sin is nigh,
and keep it still awake.

3 Almighty God of truth and love,
to me thy power impart;
the mountain from my soul remove,
the hardness from my heart.
O, may the least omission pain
my reawakened soul,
and drive me to that blood again,
which makes the wounded whole.

Poet: Charles Wesley, 1749. Meter: 8 6 8 6 (Common Meter) doubled.

In this hymn, the word *want* means "lack" or "need," not "desire." It is a confession that "I lack a principle within..." The word *filial* means "as a son or daughter." Part of sanctification is cultivating an appropriate and continuing recognition that we fail to recognize our weaknesses and our needs.

1 Jesus, my strength, my hope,
on thee I cast my care,
with humble confidence look up,
and know thou hearest my prayer.
Give me on thee to wait,
till I can all things do,
on thee, almighty to create.
almighty to renew.

2 I want a godly fear,
a quick-discerning eye
that looks to thee when sin is near,
and bids the tempter fly;
a spirit still prepared,
and armed with jealous care,
for ever standing on its guard,
and watching unto prayer.

3 I want a true regard,
a single, steady aim,
unmoved by threatening or reward,
to thee and thy great name;
a jealous, just concern
for thine immortal praise;
a pure desire that all may learn
and glorify thy grace.

4 I rest upon thy word;
thy promise is for me:
my succor and salvation, Lord,
shall surely come from thee:
but let me still abide,
nor from my hope remove;
till thou my patient spirit guide
into thy perfect love.

Poet: Charles Wesley, 1742. Meter: 6 6 8 6 (Short Meter) doubled.

Not only do we need "a principle within" (the previous hymn) but we also need "a single, steady aim" to follow God's calling for each of us.

1 When the storms of life are raging, stand by me (x2)
When the world is tossing me
like a ship upon the sea,
thou who rulest wind and water, stand by me (x2)

2 In the midst of tribulation, stand by me (x2)
When the hosts of hell assail,
and my strength begins to fail,
thou who never lost a battle: stand by me (x2)

3 In the midst of faults and failures: stand by me (x2)
When I've done the best I can,
and my friends misunderstand:
thou who knowest all about me, stand by me (x2)

4 In the midst of persecution, stand by me (x2)
When my foes in war array
undertake to stop my way,
thou who rescued Paul and Silas, stand by me (x2)

5 When I'm growing old and feeble, stand by me (x2)
When my life becomes a burden,
and I'm nearing chilly Jordan,
O thou Lily of the Valley, stand by me (x2)

Poet: Charles Albert Tindley, ca. 1906. Meter: 8 3 8 3 7 7 8 3.

Tindley's hymn addresses another aspect of Christian sanctification, asking God to sanctify us even "When the storms of life are raging..." But it is also a hymn of a Christian death, asking God to stand by us when "my life becomes a burden" and we are "nearing chilly Jordan." And there we ask God again to "stand by me."

1 If the world from you withhold of its silver and its gold,
and you have to get along with meager fare,
Just remember, in his Word, how he feeds the little bird,
take your burden to the Lord and leave it there.

> Refrain:
> Leave it there, leave it there,
> take your burden to the Lord and leave it there.
> If you trust and never doubt,
>    he will surely bring you out:
> take your burden to the Lord and leave it there.

2 If your body suffers pain and your health you can't regain,
And your soul is almost sinking in despair,
Jesus knows the pain you feel, he can save and he can heal,
Take your burden to the Lord and leave it there. [Refrain]

3 When your enemies assail and your heart begins to fail,
don't forget that God in heaven answers prayer;
he will make a way for you
and will lead you safely through:
Take your burden to the Lord and leave it there. [Refrain]

4 When your youthful days are gone
and old age is stealing on,
and your body bends beneath the weight of care,
he will never leave you then, he'll go with you to the end:
Take your burden to the Lord and leave it there. [Refrain]

Poet: Charles Albert Tindley, ca. 1906. Meter: 7 7 11 (doubled) with refrain.

Some sanctification hymns encourage us to overcome in the name of Jesus! But others like this one encourage us to take our burdens to Jesus and leave them with him. God give us the wisdom to know which way we should take!

## 105 Come, Ye Disconsolate

1 Come, ye disconsolate, where'er you languish;
come to the mercy seat, fervently kneel.
Here bring your wounded hearts, here tell your anguish;
earth has no sorrows that heaven cannot heal.

2 Joy of the desolate, light of the straying,
hope of the penitent, fadeless and pure!
Here speaks the Comforter, in mercy saying,
"Earth has no sorrows that heaven cannot cure."

3 Here see the bread of life; see waters flowing
forth from the throne of God, pure from above.
Come to the feast prepared; come, ever knowing
earth has no sorrows but heaven can remove.

Poet: Thomas Moore, 1816, as altered by Thomas Hastings, 1831. Meter: 11 10 11 10.

When we are "disconsolate" (beyond consolation) on the way to God, we need comfort. Thomas Moore's hymn offers Christ's comfort by calling us to remember that "earth has no sorrows that heaven cannot heal."

1 Must Jesus bear the cross alone
and all the world go free?
No, there's a cross for everyone,
and there's a cross for me.

2 The consecrated cross I'll bear
till death shall set me free,
and then go home my crown to wear,
for there's a crown for me.

3 Upon the crystal pavement, down
at Jesus' pierced feet,
joyful, I'll cast my golden crown
and His dear name repeat.

4 O precious cross! O glorious crown!
O resurrection day!
Ye angels, from the stars come down
and bear my soul away.

Poet: Thomas Shepherd, 1855. Meter: 8686 (Common Meter).

There was a heresy from the 1970s that we call "the prosperity gospel,"
a severe mutilation of Christian faith that pretended that Christians
could have all the blessings of health and wealth and happiness right
here and right now. Thomas Shepherd offers a realistic and faithful response: "No!" to the prosperity gospel: "there's a cross for everyone, and
there's a cross for me."

## 107 Lord, It Belongs Not to My Care

1 Lord, it belongs not to my care
whether I die or live;
to love and serve thee is my share,
and this thy grace must give.

2 If life be long, I will be glad
that I may long obey;
If short, yet why should I be sad
to soar to endless day?

3 Christ leads me through no darker rooms
than he went through before;
He that into God's kingdom comes
must enter by this door.

4 Come, Lord, when grace hath made me meet
thy blessed face to see;
for if thy work on earth be sweet,
what will thy glory be?

5 My knowledge of that life is small;
the eye of faith is dim;
But 'tis enough that Christ knows all,
and I shall be with him.

Poet: Richard Baxter, 1681. Meter: 8 6 8 6 (Common Meter).

There are things we can worry about fruitfully and things that won't do us any good at all to worry about. In the end, really, "it belongs not to my care whether I die or live." This insight from an English Puritan offers composure to a Christian. I need it.

1 We are often tossed and driven
on the restless sea of time,
somber skies and howling tempest
oft succeed a bright sunshine;
in that land of perfect day,
when the mists have rolled away,
we will understand it better by and by.

Refrain:
By and by, when the morning comes,
when the saints of God are gathered home,
we'll tell the story, how we've overcome,
for we'll understand it better by and by.

2 We are often destitute
of the things that life demands,
want of food and want of shelter,
thirsty hills and barren lands;
we are trusting in the Lord,
and according to the Word,
we will understand it better by and by. [Refrain]

3 Temptations, hidden snares,
often take us unawares,
and our hearts are made to bleed for
any thoughtless word or deed;
and we wonder why the test
when we try to do our best,
but we'll understand it better by and by. [Refrain]

Poet: Charles Albert Tindley, ca. 1906. Meter: Irregular, with refrain.

Charles Albert Tindley's hymn admits how much we don't know and encourages us to be comforted in the knowledge that "we'll understand it better by and by." Join me and Rev. Tindley in confessing how much we don't know and believing that "we'll understand it better by and by."

## 109 Jesus Calls Us O'er the Tumult

1 Jesus calls us o'er the tumult
of our life's wild, restless sea;
day by day his sweet voice soundeth,
saying, "Christian, follow me."

2 As of old the apostles heard it
by the Galilean lake,
turned from home and toil and kindred,
leaving all for Jesus' sake.

3 Jesus calls us from the worship
of the vain world's golden store,
from each idol that would keep us,
saying, "Christian, love me more."

4 In our joys and in our sorrows,
days of toil and hours of ease,
still he calls, in cares and pleasures,
"Christian, love me more than these."

5 Jesus calls us! By thy mercies,
Savior, may we hear thy call,
give our hearts to thine obedience,
serve and love thee best of all.

Poet: Cecil Frances *née* Humphries Alexander, 1852. Meter: 8 7 8 7.

A hymn celebrating St Andrew the Apostle, the second stanza originally had "As of old St Andrew heard it..." A part of sanctification is knowing the calling, the vocation, that God has for each of us.

1 "Take up thy cross," the Savior said,
"if thou wouldst my disciple be;
deny thyself, the world forsake,
and humbly follow after me."

2 Take thy your cross, let not its weight
fill thy weak spirit with alarm.
His strength shall bear thy spirit up,
and brace thy heart and nerve thy arm.

3 Take up thy cross, nor heed the shame.
nor let thy foolish pride rebel;
thy Lord for thee the cross endured
to save thy soul from death and hell.

4 Take up your cross, and follow Christ,
Nor think till death to lay it down;
For only those who bear the cross
may hope to wear the glorious crown.

Poet: Charles W. Everest, 1833. 8 8 8 8 (Long Meter).

Another forceful rejoinder to the "prosperity gospel." Nope, once again:
"Take up your cross, and follow Christ."

1 Soldiers of Christ, arise,
and put your armor on,
strong in the strength which God supplies
through his eternal Son;
strong in the Lord of hosts
and in his mighty pow'r,
who in the strength of Jesus trusts
is more than conqueror.

2 Stand then in his great might,
with all his strength endued,
and take, to aid you in the fight,
the panoply of God.
From strength to strength go on,
wrestle and fight and pray;
tread all the pow'rs of darkness down
and win the well-fought day.

3 "Prayer without ceasing, pray,"
your Captain gives the word.
His summons cheerfully obey
and call upon the Lord.
To God your every want
in instant prayer display,
pray, always pray, and never faint,
pray, without ceasing, pray.

4 From strength to strength go on,
wrestle and fight and pray,
tread all the powers of darkness down
and win the well-fought day.
Still let the spirit cry
in all his soldiers, "Come!"
till Christ the Lord descends from high
and takes the conquerors home.

Poet: Charles Wesley, 1749. Meter: 6 6 8 6 (Short Meter) doubled.

Another hymn about weird Christian soldiers who put on the armor of faith and hope and prayer, relying on God's strange peace-giving strength.

1 Stand up, stand up for Jesus,
ye soldiers of the cross;
lift high his royal banner,
it must not suffer loss.
From victory unto victory
his army he shall lead
till every foe is vanquished
and Christ is Lord indeed.

2 Stand up, stand up for Jesus,
the trumpet call obey:
Forth to the mighty conflict
in this his glorious day.
Ye that are men now serve him
against unnumbered foes:
Let courage rise with danger
and strength to strength oppose.

3 Stand up, stand up for Jesus,
stand in his strength alone;
the arm of flesh will fail you,
ye dare not trust your own.
Put on the gospel armor,
each piece put on with prayer;
where duty calls or danger,
be never wanting there.

4 Stand up, stand up for Jesus,
the strife will not be long;
this day the noise of battle,
the next, the victor's song.
To him that overcometh
a crown of life shall be;
he with the King of glory
shall reign eternally.

Poet: G. Duffield, Jr., 1858. Meter: 7 6 7 6 doubled.

Even more weird Christian soldiers who put on the armor of the gospel
(Good News!) with prayer!

## 113 Rescue the Perishing

1 1 Rescue the perishing,
care for the dying,
snatch them in pity from sin and the grave;
weep o'er the erring one, lift up the fallen,
tell them of Jesus the mighty to save.

> Refrain:
> Rescue the perishing,
> care for the dying;
> Jesus is merciful,
> Jesus will save.

2 Though they are slighting Him,
still He is waiting,
waiting the penitent child to receive;
Plead with them earnestly, plead with them gently;
he will forgive if they only believe. [Refrain]

3 Down in the human heart,
crushed by the tempter,
feelings lie buried that grace can restore;
touched by a loving heart, wakened by kindness,
chords that were broken will vibrate once more. [Refrain]

4 Rescue the perishing,
Duty demands it;
Strength for thy labor the Lord will provide;
Back to the narrow way patiently win them;
Tell the poor wanderer a Savior has died. [Refrain]

Poet: Frances Jane *née* Crosby Van Alstyne, 1869. Meter: 8 8 8 8 (Long Meter).

The path of sanctification is also a path of service. Some Christians are called by God to serve others as a life vocation, like the deacons appointed "to serve" (*diakonein*) in Acts 6:2. Frances Jane Crosby here issues the call to Christian service coupled with evangelization that is a hallmark of Wesleyan Christianity.

1 Forth in thy name, O Lord, I go,
my daily labor to pursue,
thee only thee resolved to know
in all I think or speak or do.

2 The task thy wisdom hath assigned,
O let me cheerfully fulfill;
in all my works thy presence find,
and prove thy good and perfect will.

3 Thee may I set at my right hand;
whose eyes my inmost substance see,
and labor on at thy command
and offer all my works to thee.

4 For thee delightfully employ
whate'er thy bounteous grace hath given,
and run my course with even joy,
and closely walk with thee to heaven.

Poet: Charles Wesley, 1749. Meter: 8 8 8 8 (Long Meter).

Now we're back on the journey, walking to heaven with Jesus and hopefully making the world better, more like the reign of God, along the way. Here Charles Wesley gives us words to pray for the grace, the gift, of resolution to stay on the path to God's reign.

As John Wesley lay dying on his bed on City Road in 1791, he tried repeatedly to utter "I'll praise…" "I'll praise…" Methodists in attendance knew what he was trying to sing: the great hymn of a holy Christian death in the words of a Psalm paraphrase by his older friend Isaac Watts, "I'll praise my Maker while I've breath, and when my voice is lost in death…" (see the following hymn text).

Death is not as visible today as it was to our forebears. A great deal of early Methodist piety looked forward to a holy Christian death. Death is part of life. Why did Christ have to die? The simplest answer is that for God to become fully incarnate—fully "in the flesh," fully human—God in Christ had to experience death. To be human is to die. We're all headed there.

Death is the culmination of life. Methodists keep that in mind by hymns that realistically depicted the crown of life as a holy death.

1 I'll praise my maker while I've breath,
and when my voice is lost in death,
praise shall employ my nobler powers;
my days of praise shall ne'er be past,
while life, and thought, and being last,
or immortality endures.

2 Happy the one whose hopes rely
on Israel's God who made the sky,
and earth and seas, with all their train;
his truth forever stands secure;
he saves the oppressed, he feeds the poor,
and none shall find his promise vain.

3 The LORD pours eyesight on the blind;
the LORD supports the fainting mind;
He sends the laboring conscience peace,
He helps the stranger in distress,
the widow and the fatherless,
and grants the prisoner sweet release.

4 I'll praise my God who lends me breath;
and when my voice is lost in death,
praise shall employ my nobler powers;
my days of praise shall ne'er be past,
while life and thought and being last,
or immortality endures.

Poet: Isaac Watts, 1719. Meter: 8 8 8 8 8 8.

Isaac Watts's paraphrase of the 146th Psalm became a way of teaching about a faithful Christian death. John Wesley attempted to say the words as he was dying, but could only say "I'll praise... I'll praise..."

1 Abide with me: fast falls the eventide;
the darkness deepens; Lord, with me abide.
When other helpers fail and comforts flee,
Help of the helpless, O abide with me.

2 Swift to its close ebbs out life's little day;
earth's joys grow dim, its glories pass away.
Change and decay in all around I see.
O thou who changest not, abide with me.

3 I need thy presence every passing hour.
What but thy grace can foil the tempter's power?
Who like thyself my guide and strength can be?
Through cloud and sunshine, O abide with me.

4 I fear no foe with thee at hand to bless,
ills have no weight, and tears no bitterness.
Where is death's sting? Where, grave, thy victory?
I triumph still, if thou abide with me.

5 Hold thou thy cross before my closing eyes.
Shine through the gloom and point me to the skies.
Heaven's morning breaks and earth's vain shadows flee;
in life, in death, O Lord, abide with me.

Poet: Henry F. Lyte, 1847. Meter: 10 10 10.

Henry Lyte's poem does not avoid describing the moment of death:
"Hold thou thy cross before my closing eyes." The first stanza of this
hymn is often sung by spectators at the beginning of British football
(soccer) matches, a way of calming them before the match: it's a sober-
ing song.

1 Lead, kindly light, amid the encircling gloom:
Lead thou me on!
The night is dark, and I am far from home,
Lead thou me on!
Keep thou my feet: I do not ask to see
the distant scene: one step enough for me.

2 I was not ever thus, nor prayed that thou
shouldst lead me on;
I loved to choose and see my path but now:
Lead thou me on!
I loved the garish day, and spite of fears,
pride ruled my will: remember not past years.

3 So long thy power hath blest me, sure it still
will lead me on
o'er moor and fen, o'er crag and torrent till
the night is gone.
And with the morn those angel faces smile,
which I have loved long since and lost awhile.

Poet: John Henry Cardinal Newman, 1833. Meter: 10 4 10 4 10 10.

Cardinal Newman's hymn envisions our journey to God, wandering away and then finding God's way for us, and finally awakening with Christ in heaven where we see our loved ones from whom we had been separated.

## 118 Come, Let Us Join Our Friends Above

1 Come, let us join our friends above
who have obtained the prize,
and on the eagle wings of love
to joys celestial rise.
Let saints on earth unite to sing
with those to glory gone,
for all the servants of our King
in earth and heaven are one.

2 One family we dwell in him,
one church above, beneath,
though now divided by the stream,
the narrow stream of death;
one army of the living God,
to his command we bow;
part of his host have crossed the flood,
and part are crossing now.

3 Ten thousand to their endless home
this solemn moment fly,
and we are to the margin come,
and we expect to die.
E'en now by faith we join our hands
with those that went before,
and greet the blood-besprinkled bands
on the eternal shore.

4 Our spirits too shall quickly join,
like theirs with glory crowned,
and shout to see our Captain's sign,
to hear his trumpet sound.
O that we now might grasp our Guide!
O that the word were given!
Come, Lord of Hosts, the waves divide,
and land us all in heaven.

Poet: Charles Wesley, 1759. Meter: 10 10 10 10.

We join together and sing with those who have gone before us. We sing "with angels and archangels and all the company of heaven" as we are "gathered to our people."

1 Jesus, the name high over all
in hell or earth or sky;
angels and mortals prostrate fall,
and devils fear and fly.

2 Jesus, the name to sinners dear,
the name to sinners given;
it scatters all their guilty fear,
it turns their hell to heaven.

3 O that the world might taste and see
the riches of his grace!
The arms of love that compass me
would all the world embrace.

4 Thee I shall constantly proclaim,
though earth and hell oppose;
bold to confess thy glorious Name
before a world of foes.

5 His only righteousness I show,
his saving truth proclaim;
'tis all my business here below
to cry, "Behold the Lamb!"

6 Happy, if with my latest breath
I may but gasp his name,
preach him to all, and cry in death,
"Behold, behold the Lamb!"

Poet: Charles Wesley, 1749. Meter: 8 6 8 6 (Common Meter).

The phrase "my latest breath" in the concluding stanza means "my last breath," my dying breath. It is a prayer for a faithful death in which we confess our faith in Christ who has already defeated death for us.

1 How happy every child of grace,
who knows his sins forgiven!
"This earth," he cries, "is not my place,
I seek my place in heaven:
a country far from mortal sight,
which yet by faith I see:
the land of rest, the saints' delight,
the heaven prepared for me."

2 O what a blessed hope is ours!
While here on earth we stay:
we more than taste the heavenly powers,
and antedate that day.
We feel the resurrection near,
our life in Christ concealed,
and with his glorious presence here
our earthen vessels filled.

Poet: Charles Wesley 1759. Meter: 8 6 8 6 (Common Meter) doubled.

I mentioned in the introduction that my mother had severe Alzheimer's disease. In her last years, she would casually say that she had just been over to talk to her mother, who had died more then 20 years before. On the telephone one night she told me she was sitting with her father, who had died about 40 years before. I said, "O let me talk to him." She handed off the phone and—as I had guessed—my dad answered.

My dad was very upset about this. He kept showing her photos of her parents' graves to prove to her that they were dead. But I said, "It's OK, dad. She's already beginning to live into the communion of saints." And that's what this Charles Wesley hymn is about: as we approach death, we begin even here on earth to live closer to the communion of the saints, "the land of rest ...".

The persistent message of Jesus was, "The time is fulfilled, and the kingdom of God has come near..." (St Mark 1:15). Methodist hymns celebrate and "anticipate" (look forward to) the coming reign of God.

Looking forward to the reign of God was not just a "heavenly" matter: for social-activist Methodists, preparing for the reign or "Kingdom of God" was a central theme: the earth has to be made—by God's grace—into the good place where God truly reigns. They built schools and universities and hospitals and shelters and outreach centers and other ministries grounded in their confidence that the reign of God was coming on earth.

1 All hail the power of Jesus' name!
Let angels prostrate fall.
Bring forth the royal diadem,
and crown him Lord of all.
Bring forth the royal diadem,
and crown him Lord of all!

2 Ye chosen seed of Israel's race,
ye ransomed from the fall,
hail him who saves you by his grace,
and crown him Lord of all!
Hail him who saves you by his grace,
and crown him Lord of all!

3 Let every kindred, every tribe
on this terrestrial ball
to him all majesty ascribe
and crown him Lord of all!
To him all majesty ascribe,
and crown him Lord of all!

4 Oh, that with all the sacred throng
we at his feet may fall!
We'll join the everlasting song
and crown him Lord of all.
We'll join the everlasting song
and crown him Lord of all.

Poet: Edward Perronet, 1779. Meter: 8 6 8 6 (Common Meter).

The gospel begins with Jesus preaching: "The time is fulfilled, and the kingdom of God has come near..." And Jesus taught us to pray, "Thy kingdom come, thy will be done on earth, as it is in heaven." Edward Perronet's hymn envisions the final triumph of the Reign of God over every horror, every nastiness, every crappy thing that had come before. It's about time!

1 Crown him with many crowns,
the Lamb upon his throne.
Hark! how the heavenly anthem drowns
all music but its own.
Awake, my soul, and sing
of him who died for thee,
and hail him as thy matchless King
through all eternity.

2 Crown him the Lord of life,
who triumphed o'er the grave,
and rose victorious in the strife
for those he came to save.
his glories now we sing
who died and rose on high,
who died eternal life to bring,
and lives that death may die.

3 Crown him the Lord of peace,
whose power a scepter sways
from pole to pole that wars may cease
and all be prayer and praise.
His reign shall know no end,
and round his pierced feet
fair flowers of paradise extend
their fragrance ever sweet.

4 Crown him the Lord of love;
behold his hands and side,
those wounds, yet visible above,
in beauty glorified.
All hail, Redeemer, hail!
For thou hast died for me,
thy praise and glory shall not fail
through all eternity.

Poet: Matthew Bridges, 1851. Meter: 6 6 8 6 (Common Meter), doubled.

Another hymn of the glorious triumph of the reign of God over every earthly power. Come, Lord Jesus!

1 The head that once was crowned with thorns
is crowned with glory now;
a royal diadem adorns
the mighty victor's brow.

2 The highest place that heaven affords
is his, is his by right,
the King of kings and Lord of lords,
and heaven's eternal light.

3 The joy of all who dwell above,
the joy of all below,
to whom he manifests his love,
and grants his name to know.

4 To them the cross with all its shame,
with all its grace, is given,
their name, an everlasting name,
their joy, the joy of heaven.

5 They suffer with their Lord below,
they reign with him above,
their profit and their joy to know
the mystery of his love.

6 The cross he bore is life and health,
though shame and death to him:
his people's hope, his people's wealth,
their everlasting theme.

Poet: Thomas Kelly, 1820. Meter: 8 6 8 6 (Common Meter).

Here's a Christian answer to the prosperity gospel: our everlasting "life and health" and even "wealth" is the cross that Christ bore for us. Amen! Come, Lord Jesus!

## 124  Rejoice, the Lord is King

1 Rejoice, the Lord is King!
Your Lord and King adore!
Rejoice, give thanks and sing,
and triumph evermore.
Lift up your heart,
lift up your voice!
Rejoice, again I say, rejoice!

2 Jesus, the Savior, reigns,
The God of truth and love;
when he had purged our stains,
he took his seat above;
Lift up your heart,
lift up your voice!
Rejoice, again I say, rejoice!

3 His kingdom cannot fail,
he rules o'er earth and heaven;
the keys of death and hell
are to our Jesus given:
Lift up your heart,
lift up your voice!
Rejoice, again I say, rejoice!

4 Rejoice in glorious hope!
Our Lord and judge shall come
and take his servants up
to their eternal home:
Lift up your heart,
lift up your voice!
Rejoice, again I say, rejoice!

Poet: Charles Wesley, 1746. Meter: 8 6 8 6 (Common Meter).

Composer George Frideric Handel wrote and sent to Charles Wesley a
tune specifically for this hymn text, though it has not been commonly
used by Methodists: see *United Methodist Hymnal* (1989), number 716.

1 Jesus shall reign where'er the sun
does its successive journeys run,
his kingdom stretch from shore to shore,
till moons shall wax and wane no more.

2 To him shall endless prayer be made,
and praises throng to crown his head.
His name like sweet perfume shall rise
with every morning sacrifice.

3 People and realms of every tongue
dwell on his love with sweetest song,
and infant voices shall proclaim
their early blessings on his name.

4 Blessings abound where'er he reigns:
the prisoners leap to lose their chains,
the weary find eternal rest,
and all who suffer want are blest.

5 Let every creature rise and bring
honors peculiar to our King,
angels descend with songs again,
and earth repeat the loud amen.

Poet: Isaac Watts, 1719. Meter: 8 8 8 8 (Long Meter).

Isaac Watts offers his own hymn of the final reign of Christ: "the prisoners leap to lose their chains, the weary find eternal rest, and all who
suffer want [need] are blest!" Come, Lord Jesus!

1 A charge to keep I have,
a God to glorify,
a never-dying soul to save,
and fit it for the sky.

2 To serve the present age,
my calling to fulfill,
O may it all my powers engage
to do my Master's will!

3 Arm me with jealous care
as in thy sight to live,
and O! thy servant, Lord, prepare
a strict account to give!

4 Help me to watch and pray,
and on thyself rely,
assured, if I my trust betray,
I shall forever die.

Charles Wesley, 1762. Meter: 6 6 8 6 (Short Meter).

This hymn is a persistent element of Methodist culture, especially associated with the conclusion of an annual conference after all the appointments for the coming year have been read. Now "A charge to keep I have…"! Now "a charge to keep" *we* have!

# Index